The Interviewer's Handbook

The Interviewer's Handbook

A Guerrilla Guide
Techniques & Tactics for Reporters & Writers

BY JOHN BRADY

The Writer Books

The Writer Books is an imprint of Kalmbach Trade Press, a division of Kalmbach Publishing Co. These books are distributed to the book trade by Watson-Guptill.

For all other inquiries, including individual orders or details on special quantity discounts for groups or conferences, contact:

Kalmbach Publishing Co.
21027 Crossroads Circle
Waukesha, WI 53187
(800) 533-6644

Visit our website at http://www.thewriterbooks.com.
Secure online ordering available.

For feedback on this or any other title by The Writer Books, contact us at this e-mail address: writerbooks@kalmbach.com.

Printed in Canada

04 05 06 07 08 09 10 11 12   10 9 8 7 6 5 4 3 2 1

Publisher's Cataloging-in-Publication

    Brady, John Joseph, 1942-
      The interviewer's handbook : a guerrilla guide :
(techniques and tactics for reporters and writers) / by
John Brady.
      p. cm.
      Includes bibliographical references and index.
      ISBN 0-87116-205-9

      1. Interviewing in journalism—Handbooks, manuals,
etc. I. Title

    PN4784.I6B675 2004   070.4'3
                      QBI04-200036

Cover design by Lisa Bergman
Cover photo by Getty Images
Author photo by Steve Marsel

Dedicated to

the Memory of

TOM HUNTER

Outstanding Interviewer,

Powerful Writing Coach,

Dear Friend

CONTENTS

This book began in Waukesha, Wisconsin, where I was giving a workshop on interviewing a few seasons ago for editors at the Kalmbach Publishing Co. During a break in the afternoon program, I chatted with Phil Martin, an editor in the books department. He held a well-thumbed copy of my book, *The Craft of Interviewing*, as we spoke.

"Ever think of doing a new book on interviewing?" he asked. "Something like a guerrilla guide?"

"All the time," I said. "A lot has happened in the field. And I know a lot of tactics that they don't teach you in journalism school."

And so began a dialogue that led to what you now hold in your hand—a guerrilla guide dedicated to the proposition that good stories are built upon solid interviewing. Interviews are to reporting what verbs are to sentences. Without the power of a verb, a sentence cannot deliver a complete thought. No verb, no sentence. Likewise, no interviews, no story.

This handbook is a gathering of tips and techniques on how to overcome obstacles and get ahead in the artful craft of interviewing. It is based upon lessons I have gained from some thirty years of interviewing, writing and editing stories for publication; and interacting with editors, writers, public-relations personnel, broadcasters, and others who have agreed to share their insights and trade secrets.

Has interviewing changed since *The Craft of Interviewing* was published in 1976? I answer with an unequivocating yes and no. Today many of the problems—and the solutions—are the same. Only different.

In 1976, there were no PCs or Macs. The thought of using a computer and online databases to conduct speedy background research on a potential interview subject seemed like something reserved for the CIA.

Now we have computer-assisted reporting, which is helpful when doing research. But the rest of the story still calls for interviewing skills. When veteran newspaper and magazine journalist John Lombardi was asked recently what advice he would give young journalists, he replied:

"Get out of the office. Don't be satisfied with database reporting. You have to humanize the story. Facts by themselves can be very limiting."

We live in the age of the sound bite and the fury. In broadcasting, skillful interviewers wield more power than ever. Certainly, many interviewers today are better known than their subjects. They have enormous powers of intimidation over a conversation, usually for broadcast, often for print. We have seen Ted Koppel on the cover of *Newsweek*, Dan Rather on the cover of *Time* magazine.

We have also seen, on the flip side of celebrity, Jiminy Glick, the world's worst celebrity interviewer, as portrayed by Martin Short in a fat suit. Jiminy is an extreme case, of course, interrupting subjects all the time, even taking cell-phone calls during the interview.

"He is the world's worst, most self-involved interviewer," says Short, who based the character on his recollection of an interview he suffered through in his early days.

In book publishing, the rise of the "as-told-to" book has made it more important (and lucrative) for writers to develop good listening and good questioning techniques. *People* magazine's success (and the emergence of celebrity journalism in all categories, not just showbiz) indicates that the reading public never tires of a well-written profile, generously sprinkled with lively quotes. Newspapers, too, are moving away from the old "five *W*s and an *H*" approach to stories; they are using more aggressive interviewing and reporting techniques to tell a story like it truly is.

Another development is the skyrocketing frequency of telephone and online interviews, which has given rise to a need for new rules on interview etiquette and strategies. How do you breathe life and personality into an interview done completely on the phone?

And then we have the emergence of PR as a powerful influence on the field. Wise to the ways of reporters, many interview subjects today are more defensive and wary than they used to be. Many receive briefings from PR intermediaries before—or during—an interview. Others have learned how to manipulate and control the interview to avoid incriminating topics.

There is also the sticky matter of legal considerations. We live in litigious times, and libel legislation—some federal, some peculiar to individual states—has made a minefield of the interviewer's turf. How can an interviewer get a great story and avoid being blasted by a lawsuit in the process?

In interviewing, more than in any other trade, there are still no easy answers. In the age of "reality TV," there is no moral outrage at invading a person's privacy; indeed, there is gleeful delight in crashing someone's privacy, being the cause of embarrassment. At the same time, public repulsion has tempered certain TV practices such as the "ambush interview," in which camera crews chase after news subjects who clearly do not want to talk. In 1982 an ABC News poll showed that six of every ten Americans said they favor a law barring TV reporters from questioning people who don't want to be interviewed. (Lest we forget, a reluctant interviewee is entitled to freedom from the press.)

Much of the antipathy toward the media is a side-effect of hostile interviewing and the attitude in some quarters of journalism that it's better to be first than to be right. Consider the last days of baseball legend Joe DiMaggio, whose name had appeared in reports regularly when he entered a Florida hospital for treatment of pneumonia.

When NBC broke the news of his death on January 24, 1999, with a "crawl" across the bottom of America's television screens, the news was a shock, but no surprise to viewers—except to Joe DiMaggio, who watched the bulletin while resting quietly. A few weeks previous, when he woke from a coma, DiMaggio's first words were to tell his doctor to stop speaking to the press. (*Sports Illustrated* columnist and wag Steve Rushin noted that "a nation that once asked, 'Where have you gone, Joe DiMaggio?' was left to wonder . . . '*Have* you gone, Joe DiMaggio?'")

"The nineteenth century was the era of the novelist," James Reston once observed. "The twentieth is the era of the journalist."

Now, at the outset of the twenty-first century, most of what reporters give their audiences comes from listening closely to what others have to say. Journalism has been described as the art of making friends quickly. Interviewers have this gift to an amazing degree. The interview is key to quotes often heard 'round the world.

Whether you are a newcomer to the interviewing wars or a veteran, we are in this business of gathering and disseminating information together. It's our task to find the key to opening the reluctant ones up, to get them talking about themselves honestly, engagingly, and quotefully. And while bad things often happen to good interviewers, we have come to learn that most subjects like to talk about themselves. Only, some of them don't know it yet.

In this artful craft, there are no bad interviews, ultimately. Interviewers learn through trial and terror. Failure enables you to recognize a mistake when you encounter it again. We listen, revisit, and moan at missed opportunities . . . and move on. This spirit is best expressed by Susan Stamberg, the award-winning National Public Radio correspondent, who did an estimated 35,000 interviews during her first thirty years on the job, and is still going strong.

And what's her favorite interview?

"The next one!"

John Brady
Bradybrady@aol.com

CHAPTER 1

Getting to Yes

In the good old days of tabloid journalism, when legendary reporters like Roger Birtwell were looking for scoops, getting the interview was a kinder and gentler pursuit. Birtwell, who did time on several of the New York dailies, beat his competition in 1930 by simply rowing out to the yacht of Cornelius Vanderbilt, whereupon the industrialist, thinking the visiting oarsman was a friend, helped him aboard the *Shamrock V*—and gave him a most gracious interview.

On another occasion, Birtwell went to Connecticut to get the story on Yale halfback Albie Booth, who was dying after the 1931 Harvard-Yale game. (Football was a lot tougher in those days.) The press was barred, but Birtwell—tall, dignified, carrying a black case—went to the kitchen entrance, where employees thought he was a doctor heading for the halfback's room. The reporter got the interview . . . and wrote the story on the typewriter in his black case.

Today, things are considerably different—and more difficult—for the interviewer, right? That's the theory, anyway.

Chicago Sun-Times reporter Mike Anderson was doing a story on a school for autistic children, and he could not get in to see the principal until he posed as a parent. "I just grabbed a random kid by the hand and walked inside," he said.

"Once in, I asked for directions to the principal's office and went there. I got inside his office, slammed the door shut and whipped out a press pass, and said, 'I have some questions to ask you.' He was trapped."

A few pennants ago, when Yankees' owner George Steinbrenner flew into New York the day before his team announced the signing of Reggie Jackson, Steinbrenner was startled to be trapped at LaGuardia by NBC Sports.

"How'd you know when I was coming in?" he inquired.

An NBC staffer, who knew that Steinbrenner was at his Florida home, had called each airline that flew from Tampa to New York, saying, "This is George Steinbrenner. I'd like to confirm my reservation on your flight to New York this afternoon."

When Delta Air Lines cheerfully confirmed the reservation, NBC knew which flight to meet with the microphones. Moreover, when Steinbrenner said, off mike, that Jackson would be flying in that night or early the next morning, the same method of checking produced confirmation from American Airlines: Mr. R. Jackson would be landing at JFK shortly after midnight. Again, NBC was the greeting committee.

In another case, a magazine staff writer was getting nowhere in his efforts to interview a key source for his story. As the deadline drew near, he decided to turn the chore over to a departmental secretary who was known for her persistence and ingenuity. She phoned the source's secretary and asked to speak with the boss.

"Who's calling?" asked the intermediary.

"His girlfriend," replied the secretary.

The boss got on the line immediately, and he was turned over to the writer. He did not hang up.

Welcome to the Media Age, when nearly everyone feels entitled to their fifteen minutes of celebritydom. Of course, the subject can refuse to talk. Remember, a reluctant interviewee is entitled to freedom from the press. Subjects worth talking to who have even a pinch of experience must be coddled and coaxed. Business leaders are famous. Lawyers are famous. Scientists are famous. All of a sudden, everyone is in the fame game.

Even old reliables become irresolvables when they wake up and find themselves just the least bit famous. According to gonzo journalist Hunter Thompson, the Hell's Angels were an undistinguished group of motorcycle freaks until California's attorney general issued an inflated report of their activities, and suddenly, "The whole scene changed in a flash. One day they were a gang of bums, scratching for any hard dollar . . . and 24 hours later they were dealing with reporters, photographers, freelance writers and all kinds of showbiz hustlers talking big money. They developed a prima-donna complex, demanding cash contributions (to confound the Internal Revenue Service) in return for photos and interviews."

Freelance writer Thomas Fields-Meyer, working on an *Esquire* profile of comic Conan O'Brien as he waited to see whether he would be David Letterman's replacement on the *Late Night Show*, found himself caught in the swirl of the suddenly famous subject. "I talked to him the day before he got the news from NBC," said Fields-Meyer, who attended Harvard the same time as O'Brien, "and he had all the time in the world.

"The next day, though, he ripped his answering machine out of the wall."

In my own travels and travails as a writer and magazine journalist, I have done, for better and for worse, a few thousand interviews. Subjects have ranged from a heart-transplant patient who claimed to have had a religious "change of heart" as a result of his operation to Jerry Springer, the controversial TV host whom I suspected of having a heart of pure sleaze when I sat down to interview him for *Playboy* magazine.

Actually, Springer turned out to be a princely sort of fellow, whereas the transplantee (who kept sneaking cigarettes, against doctor's orders) wondered how much he would be paid for cooperating with the project. I said I would get back to him on that.

In both instances—and in the other few thousand interviews as well—the most important thing was gaining access to my subject: Being There, ready to start the interview. Even if a subject has some last-minute reservations or requests, the key to success in this business is what Barbara Walters calls "gets." She means getting a subject, especially one in demand, to say "Yes, I will talk with you."

Getting to Yes with a subject, therefore, should never be considered an easy task. Even when approaching unknown subjects, the getting can be tough. Then there are cases like Tony Stewart, one of NASCAR racing's biggest stars, who has been sighted brooding at press briefings in a T-shirt that announced: You have the right to remain silent—Anything you say will be misquoted and used against you.

On another occasion, a reporter approached Stewart for a comment after a race when the driver was angered by what he thought was an unfair ruling by NASCAR officials. Stewart swatted a tape recorder out of the interviewer's hand, then kicked it under a truck.

Garry Shandling would only speak to Tad Friend of *Esquire* magazine in character, that character being fictional talk-show host Larry Sanders (of Shandling's *Larry Sanders Show*). "I would ask Garry a question," Friend said, "and he would then tell me to ask him the same question again but to Larry. It was kind of like dealing with the Smothers Brothers—only funny."

And singer Neil Young refused to give an interview to *Rolling Stone*, saying, of course, that he didn't like the way the magazine smelled.

Gay Talese once observed that the journalist is often "the important ally of the ambitious . . . a lamplighter for stars." Both interviewer and subject often go away with something for their efforts. Sports interviews are usually easy to obtain because sports heroes are dependent on public favor. At one point in a media blitz, Madonna gave an "exclusive" interview to just about every publication but *Supermarket News*. Still, there are always some unreachables out there, of course; or those who fancy themselves as such.

In order to get a rare interview with reclusive author J. D. Salinger, writer Betty Eppes of the *Baton Rouge Sunday Advocate* journeyed all the way to Cornish, New Hampshire. There, she found that "Whenever I mentioned his name, the whole town froze over." Salinger had not given an interview since he spoke with a high-school reporter twenty years earlier, and the townspeople respected his feelings.

Finally, Eppes befriended a store owner who knew Salinger's unlisted phone number. She soon found herself on the phone with the author's housekeeper, who revealed that the only way to reach Salinger was to leave a note at the post office. Eppes did so, saying she would wait for him for thirty minutes the next morning.

On Friday morning, Salinger showed up.

"For twenty-seven minutes, he answered everything I asked—in pure Zen," reported Eppes.

"There is so much that cannot be known," said Salinger regarding his choice of material. "We each have to find our way. We make decisions along the way, but the subject may choose the writer."

Salinger told the interviewer that he was writing regularly, but had no plans to publish soon.

"Sometimes I almost wish I'd never published," he added.

After entertainment writer Ernie Santosuosso reviewed the little-known Osmond Brothers during one of their early appearances in Boston, the boys surprised the *Boston Globe* reporter at lunch the next day.

"Though evidently on their way up, they were amiable and civilized," he said after the unexpected visit.

But two years later, at a capacity Boston Garden turnout, Santosuosso was told: "Sorry, no interviews."

In other words, getting interviews can be, at best, uncertain. A sense of timing helps. Perhaps the uncertainty of it all is what keeps a good interviewer going. Nevertheless, we can learn a great deal about getting interviews from the experiences of others.

If it is an impromptu situation with someone who is famous or powerful or both, use patience. One doesn't enter Miles Davis's dressing room before a performance, for instance, and ask him what he is going to play. Ernie Santosuosso did, and Davis growled at him: "Why in the hell don't you just listen to the music?"

The writer beat a hasty retreat to a table where he sat through a set, and then later joined the Columbia Records' promotion director in Davis's dressing room.

"I had only my own naiveté to blame," recalled Santosuosso. "I was still wary as the trumpet star told me to sit down and get on with the interview. As matters turned out, it was a most satisfying interview because Davis gave direct, colorful answers to my questions. I asked why he persisted in changing his music. Fixing me with an unblinking stare, Davis said: 'I'd rather be dead than stay the same.' Inquiring into his then reluctance to play jazz festivals, I mentioned that Dizzy Gillespie performed in them because the job enabled him to eat. Davis's terse reply: 'Why doesn't Dizzy buy a Stop-and-Shop, then?'"

The initial phone-call query

The process of opening the door often begins with a phone call.

"I usually open the initial phone call with some phraseology as this," says author Max Gunther.

> Mr. Jones? My name is Max Gunther.
> I'm a writer, and I'm working on a book about such-and-such.
> Since you're in the this-and-that business, I thought maybe
> you could give me a little information.

This approach is an effective door-opener, but it also raises questions in the mind of prospective interviewee Jones. "My job now is to put all these mysteries to rest in Jones's mind, so that he sees exactly where he stands in relation to me and my project," says Gunther.

"I tell him everything I think he might want to know. The object is to make me something other than a total stranger. I tell him who will publish the book, if I know that fact—or who I hope will publish it, if I am in a preliminary outline-writing or selling phase of the project.

"I tell him about other people in his trade or profession whom I've interviewed or plan to interview. I explain why I've singled him out. I say precisely why I think he will be helpful and precisely what aspects of the book's subject I want him to talk about.

"By the time I finish, if I have done it right, Jones is relaxed. I am no longer a stranger. I am an amiable fellow asking a perfectly reasonable favor—the granting of which, from Jones's point-of-view, promises to be fun.

"As soon as I hear the puzzlement vanish from Jones's voice, I ask him to set an hour and date for the interview."

If you call during lunch, you may even find that the president is in and eating at his or her desk. Many celebrities and executives boast that they answer their own phones. A Blue Chip Marketing Group survey indicates that while most executives see only 10 percent of their mail, some 50 percent take unsolicited calls.

Boston Globe business writer Alex Beam did a column on well-known people who answer their own phones—and others who say that they do when in fact they don't. When Beam dialed essayist Andy Rooney at CBS headquarters in New York, the curmudgeon's assistant, Jane, picked up the line. Then Rooney came on, explaining that the younger operators at CBS don't put calls through on his personal lines, which miffed him.

"I can get rid of a call quicker than Jane can," he explained.

The next day Beam dialed Rooney on his private line, and the gravelly voiced pundit picked it right up. "And he got rid of the call quickly, too," said Beam.

If you want to talk to someone at the office, call during business hours. It helps to find out if your subject-to-be is a "morning" or "afternoon" person.

If you have his or her home phone, asking for an interview is usually best done on the weekend. To reach a well-known subject, getting a home number gives you the advantage of not having to work your way through intermediaries at the office.

How can you find home phone numbers?

- Make the phone directory your first stop.

- Then, *Who's Who in America* also lists home addresses for many noted people, as do directories for trade and professional organizations.

- If your subject has written a book, publicity directors at publishing companies may help put you in touch.

- Talent agents or public-relations agents will also often help you get a home number, even if it is unlisted, if you are on assignment for a prominent magazine or newspaper.

If you call a subject in the evening, never do so later than nine o'clock, unless you have been expressly told otherwise. Calls to the home may be considered hostile or intrusive, of course, and subject to various brush-off techniques. Disney studio head Michael Eisner, for instance, has been known to pose as a non-English-speaking houseman when reporters reach him at home.

The instant yes

If you call, thinking you will set up an interview for, oh, next week or so, when it's convenient for you—be ready to do an interview on the spot. Remember, the subject controls the timetable.

Erika Isler's first assignment as a cub reporter for *Magazine Week* was to track down "a company spokesperson" at Forbes Inc. to interview for details on a new square-shaped magazine to be called *Egg*. She called Forbes and waited. A few hours later she nearly fell off her chair when she received a call from the most official source available: Malcolm Forbes himself was on the line, ready to hold forth.

With lesser-known subjects, it is even more likely that when you call to ask for an interview, you may find yourself talking to a very flattered and willing subject. This is especially true if you call an expert at an institution that is hundreds or even thousands of miles away. After all, you have gone to some trouble to track her or him down—and everybody likes being wanted. Don't assume you will have time to arrange an interview for next week, or even tomorrow. The good doctor may be off to a conference in Zurich where he is delivering a paper, and then he is off to Zambia for six months of research—so it's today or never.

Have a few topics in mind. Be prepared to at least start the interview on the spot.

Going through intermediaries

The fastest way to an interviewee's heart is often through an intermediary. "If I had the choice to get friendly with the wife or the secretary to get information," said the late, great interviewer Alex Haley, "I'd take the secretary every time. They know much more about the man—for the interviewer, anyhow. They can also tell you how best to approach their boss —how he flows best."

In the age of interview anxiety, some receptionists may even flinch at the word *interview*. It conjures up images of a police grilling, a job interview (or worse, an exit interview if a job didn't work out), or someone from *Sixty Minutes* shoving a mike in their direction and asking uncomfortable questions about Mafia connections.

If you suspect that such anxiety is in the air, don't even use the dreaded *i*-word when making your initial approach. Instead of saying "interview," say instead "information." Try something like:

> I wonder if you could help me with some information for a
> story I'm working on for *Widget Monthly*, Mr. Hagedorn.

Make it clear that you are doing work for a publication—it's not for a student term paper. But sidestep interview anxiety by making it a helpful search for information.

A basic rule to remember when trying to get past any intermediary: never accept a no from someone who can't give you a yes. In any organization, many people can say no; few can say yes. It can be someone as basic as a receptionist (labeled "Rejectionist" in a witty *New Yorker* cartoon by Robert Mankoff).

If you run into someone who is an unhelpful no-sayer, try to get an answer to this question:

> Who else, beside yourself, is involved in access to Mr.
> Hagedorn?

From the reply, you can usually judge how weighty the interference is, and then pursue an alternate route.

When you leave a message with an intermediary, leave more than your name and number—unless you are trying to reach a background source who does not want to be affiliated with you.

> I'm doing a story on widgets, and several of my sources have
> mentioned that Mr. Hagedorn is an expert on Australian imports.
> I'd like to arrange a meeting with him.

That sort of approach makes the intermediary feel like a bearer of good news as opposed to feeling like a mere messenger.

Linda Konner, author of *How to Be Successfully Published in Magazines* (St. Martin's Press), says that treating a secretary or assistant well makes good business sense. "I never ask if the person answering the phone is

So-and-So's secretary," she says. Instead, she asks, "Do you work with (not for) So-and-So?"

"I treat him with respect and with the attitude that I'd really like his help," she adds. "Then, if we've been talking for more than a sentence or two, I'll ask his name so I can start getting into the habit of using it in future conversations. Needless to say, the call is liberally sprinkled with 'please' and 'thank you.'"

If your subject is unavailable, tell the assistant that you will call back—and ask for his or her name. Enter it in your story file, and when you call back, use it.

> Hi, Doreen. This is Jack Brady again.
> Is Mr. Hagedorn available?

Remember that word: *available*. Several things are happening here. First, you are addressing the assistant by name. That connotes respect, attention to detail, and a personal touch in the indifferent world of commerce. This friendly approach can move you to the front of the row in an assistant's list of options for Mr. Hagedorn's review.

Second, you are asking if the boss is available.

Not, "Is he in?"

Not, "May I speak with him?"

Is he available? gives Doreen lots of room to handle the request. He may be in, but not available at the moment. He may be in, but unable to speak with you as he is on the other line. Either way, *available* establishes a link between you and Hagedorn's intermediary, as you both work on this little problem of his availability.

Finally, try to enlist the secretary as an ally. Sometimes a straightforward appeal to the intermediary can get him or her on your side.

> Can you help me?

This plea is as forthright as it gets. In one case, for instance, after being put off for several days, a journalist finally asked the busy businessman's secretary, "What am I doing wrong?"

Within an hour, he was talking to the boss.

References and personal connections

Often, all you need is a reference, an introduction, or a personal link to a hard-to-get interview subject.

When a surveillance camera caught Madelyne Gorman Toogood slamming her four-year-old daughter into the back seat of an SUV in a shopping center near South Bend, Indiana, the footage was broadcast nationwide. We soon learned that Toogood belonged to a tight-lipped clan called the Irish Travelers, with outposts in Texas and southern communities. Travelers distrusted outsiders, an attitude shaped by their people's history of persecution in Ireland, where they were seen as an itinerant underclass. In the United States, they were often taunted as gypsies.

Lynne Duke of the *Washington Post* broke through clan secrecy to write a revealing profile of the Travelers in "a puzzling little community of trailer homes, Cadillacs, mini-mansions, and kissing cousins" in Edgefield County, South Carolina. Clan member Rose Kathy Sherlock broke a longstanding taboo by just talking to a stranger.

"We're like any other community, and in any other neighborhood there's good and bad," said Sherlock. "We don't like to speak out. We stay to ourselves."

Why did she open up to Duke?

"She's talking to a reporter only because a trusted friend has come along for the interview," wrote Duke.

That's the key word: *trust*. In selling interviews, as in selling anything, nice guys finish first if they can engender trust. According to one survey that queried over 200,000 customers, the key to closing the deal is to be able to trust that the salesperson will do what he says he will do.

Networking

Networking is an ideal way to pyramid your way to the top. In fact, it may be as old as the pyramids. The domino theory of networking—using one interview to obtain an interview with a more reluctant subject—can be traced back to at least 1904, when journalist Isaac Marcosson was asked by his editor to get statements from every member of Teddy Roosevelt's cabinet.

The reporter concentrated his initial effort on Paul Morton, Secretary of the Navy. "I knew that he was a novice to Washington official life," recalled the interviewer.

Once Morton agreed, then "it was comparatively easy to convince his colleagues," said Marcosson. "When they shied, I simply said: 'You do not want the Navy Department to get all the publicity, do you?' It went home every time."

Hard-to-get subjects at the top of the interview pyramid are often beholden to subjects on lower or lateral levels of power and persuasion. Shana Alexander found herself in this quandary while working on a profile of actor Tony Curtis for *Life* magazine. Curtis's agent at the time was Lew Wasserman, the powerful head of MCA and widely considered to be the smartest man in Hollywood.

"He was also the most inaccessible," reflected Alexander, who spent weeks with Curtis in a marathon series of interviews that left her feeling that she knew more about the actor than his psychiatrist did. Still, no Wasserman. In fact, the agent was so unreachable that when *Fortune* magazine sent a task force of reporters from New York to Hollywood to do a big takeout on MCA, he would not even return their calls.

One morning, toward the end of their marathon, the writer arrived at the actor's house, notebook in hand, and Curtis said, "You know, Shana, I've been thinking. Maybe you should talk to some other people about me. To get a more rounded perspective."

Curtis handed Alexander a typewritten list of some twenty names. At the head of the list was Lew Wasserman.

"Jeez, Tony, I know Wasserman won't see me," said Alexander weakly. "He hates reporters."

Curtis picked up the phone. "Lew, there's this girl here doing a big story about me for *Life* magazine, and would you . . ." A moment later the actor hung up the phone, grinned, and said: "Tomorrow morning, ten o'clock."

But don't wait for your subject to type a list of other people. Draft one yourself, and include a few of the hard-to-get types. If you are doing a favor for your subject, he may be able to ease your way in return by asking a friend to do a favor.

Journalist David Halberstam once obtained an interview with the elusive Ted Williams by using his friendly relationship with another elusive subject, basketball coach Bobby Knight. "The fact that someone such as Mr. Knight recommended me as a worthy reporter-historian to Mr. Williams had weighed heavily in my favor," said Halberstam later. In his account, he noted that "Mr. Williams was reported to have said that if Mr. Knight gave his goddamn approval, why that was goddamn good enough for Mr. Williams."

The author flew down to Florida where he met Williams at eight the next morning at a motel. "Mr. Williams took me to his house and granted me that agreed-upon interview. The interview with Mr. Williams, who is enthusiastic about whatever he undertakes, was exceptional. Not only did he answer my questions with great candor, but he also managed to give me several demonstrations of correct batting procedures."

The interview took up most of the day, concluding in dinner that night. "We had been together twelve hours and he was everything I had always hoped he would be," reflected Halberstam. "I considered it to be one of the happiest days in my life."

Working your way up the ladder

Sometimes you can get reluctant interviewees to talk to you by smoking 'em out. In practice, this often means starting small, then working your way to the top.

The early interviews often serve as good preparation for the eventual interview with the company president, whom you want to talk to as a principal actor, not as a fact-checker. By learning how the business is run from the lower-ranking employees, you can concentrate on the more important topics—company strategies and decision making—when talking with the person on top. From the CEO, you don't want to know when the widget division was acquired; instead, you want expert opinions and anecdotal recollections of battlefield business experience.

With his definitive two-part biography, Peter Guralnick did for Elvis Presley what Boswell did for Dr. Johnson. Along the way, Guralnick learned the value of working his way from one source to the next: how patience—and persistence—could lead to key interviews.

Dixie Locke, for instance, was Elvis's first girlfriend, in 1954–1955. But she didn't do interviews, saying she didn't want to cheapen the memory of their love, or open her private life to public scrutiny. But then a common friend introduced her to Peter Guralnick in 1988, and the biographer's gentle campaign began.

"You want to have enough contact so that people remember you," said Guralnick. "You don't want to have so much contact that you're a pest. Maybe I was a pest, but I tried not to be."

He called Dixie whenever he was in Memphis, and he would go to the church where she worked and say hello. Finally, after two years, they sat down with a tape recorder in the basement of the same church Dixie and Elvis attended as teenagers, and she told him the entire story, from the night she met Elvis at the Rainbow Rollerdrome to the last time she saw him, at Graceland, the day after his mother's funeral.

The interview became a cornerstone in Guralnick's research. "I think it was one of the most emotional interviews I've ever done," he said.

"She was so honest, and she told the story so eloquently. Afterward, it was almost as if we both slunk away from the church basement like we had done something wrong. Because it had that degree—I think at least from my perspective—it had that degree of emotional investment."

Celebrity status for interviewers

Of course, if you are a celebrity yourself (as is David Halberstam, the writer who landed the interview with Ted Williams), that can help you get to yes in high places. In fact, high-profile interviewers may be as well or even better known than the people they interview. One survey indicated that Barbara Walters had a name recognition of 94%—higher than politicians, even the president.

In the 1960s, Richard Nixon practiced law in New York City, where he was a fan of the New York Giants football team. He often attended postgame parties at celebrated halfback Frank Gifford's place. In 1971, Roone Arledge, president of ABC Sports, hired Gifford to announce the Hall of Fame exhibition football game in Canton, Ohio.

When Richard Nixon decided to drop in on the game, suddenly Gifford's first assignment was to interview the president of the United States.

Minutes before the broadcast, Nixon told Arledge what a fan he had been of the Giants back when Gifford embodied the team.

"I'm sure Frank would remember me," he said.

Bob Woodward is known as the reporter, along with Carl Bernstein, who cracked the Watergate case. When Woodward started doing research for a book about the late John Belushi, the comedian's agent, Bernie Brillstein, was thrilled when Belushi's widow called Brillstein and encouraged him to talk to Bob.

"We went to lunch. I gave him access to files. I gave him pictures. He got me to tell him things I would never have told anyone else," said Brillstein.

The book, *Wired*, however, was not exactly a celebration of Belushi; rather, it chronicled Belushi's life in excruciating detail, including many drug parties. "I guess maybe I thought I was getting Robert Redford or something. Bob Woodward was one of my heroes, but he turned out to be one of the greatest disappointments of my life," admitted Brillstein.

"Movie people consider journalists, particularly somebody of Bob's stature, celebrities," said Robert Markowitz, a Hollywood friend of Woodward. "They felt they were talking to someone in the same galaxy. They thought he would filter out some of the things they said. Bob assumed that because of his body of work and who he was, they'd understand what he was doing. But they were incredibly naive."

Presenting yourself

Your credentials are important. Be prepared to present a business card, a press card, a letter of assignment from your editor, a copy of the publication, even sample clips, when it's time to get through security to talk to your subject. Before consenting to an interview, many subjects will ask themselves, "Do I want to appear in this publication and seemingly endorse it with my presence?"

Obviously, it helps to work for a publication known in your field. This enables you to open doors, to have your phone messages returned. It stretches your reach as an interviewer. But never assume the subject will know you or your work. Ernest Hemingway was once ushered into the

Yankees' clubhouse and introduced to Yogi Berra as a writer.

"Yeah," said Berra, "what paper do you write for?"

In most cases, it is the publication's name that has the real clout. Enough clout can even save an interviewer's life. *Time* magazine reporter James Wilde spent thirty years reporting on wars from Vietnam, Africa, and the Middle East. Still, one of his most terrifying moments occurred not in some far-off jungle, but in New York City when he was interviewing a fourteen-year-old mugger known as Baby Love. When the interview was over, Wilde held out his hand to say goodbye and the punk drew a Magnum on him.

"If you kill me, you won't get into *Time*," warned the reporter.

"Right on, Mr. James, right on," said Baby Love—and put the gun away.

In his capacity as press spokesman for the Reagan administration, Larry Speakes was accused from time to time of catering to the big newspapers.

"I would never have admitted it publicly, but obviously we did, because the *Washington Post* and the *New York Times* had the most influence with opinion-makers," he confessed after leaving office. After the *Post* and the *Times*, Speakes gave priority to the wire services, which could not be ignored "for their influence in Middle America." Still, because they had "almost no influence in Washington," they were "reduced almost to handout organizations. There was seldom a scoop on any wire."

So don't act like you are from the *New York Times* if you aren't. On the other hand, if you *are* from the *New York Times*, enjoy the special treatment. On his last working day there, former editor A. M. Rosenthal reflected on his life and *Times* clout: "Arrive in a foreign capital for the first time, call a government minister, and give just your name. Ensues iciness. But add 'of the *New York Times*,' and you *expect* to be invited right over and usually are; nice."

Similarly, freelancer Larry Miller recalled, "When I worked for the *New York Times*, I would call for interviews and be told that Mr. X was in conference and asked who was calling. I would reply, 'Larry Miller from the *New York Times*,' and the response would be instantaneous: 'Oh, just a moment, please, Mr. Miller, and Mr. X will be right with you.'"

As a freelancer working on other assignments, Miller found that he had to use credentials wherever he could find them. "Even though you may not be on a publication's staff, say, 'I'm doing an article for *Boys' Life*—or *Family Weekly* or *Sport* or whatever the magazine or newspaper is. Ask your editor if you can identify yourself as a contributor; this sounds impressive and to most people implies that you're on staff.

"And stress the fact that the article has been definitely assigned, that you are not merely prospecting."

When Miller called Dr. Joyce Brothers for an interview, her response was frank: "Is this an assignment from the magazine?

"It is? Okay, I'll talk to you."

Of course, you can't always be certain that the publication you are touting will be well received by the wary subject. *New York* magazine columnist Michael Wolff once called Arthur Sulzberger, Jr., publisher of the *New York Times*, and asked if he would do a formal sit-down interview.

Sulzberger said he would think about it.

A few days later, he said, "I've really thought about it, and you know why I don't want to do it? Because I hate *New York* magazine."

Occasionally, a writer can obtain an interview with a hard-to-get subject with a letter of introduction from someone who will vouch for the interviewer's work. Film director John Huston wrote such a letter for biographer Lawrence Grobel; it enabled the journalist to obtain interviews with many people who usually don't talk to writers. Huston's cooperation and artistic trust were exceptional in a field known for paranoia.

"He wanted nothing in return except for me to write the best book I could. He didn't want to see the manuscript when it was done and didn't think any member of his family should either," wrote Grobel.

"It was a bond of trust. He trusted that I would tell his family's story as honestly as I could, without glossing over the sensitive parts."

Establishing expectations

You may have to arrange or agree to ground rules as a basis for a subject's consent. These can be confining for the interviewer and self-serving for the subject, but if the interview is important enough, you may have little choice but to agree to them, or to walk away from the project.

"The straight Q&A is usually done with celebrities and personalities—who often require prepared questions since their time is usually more limited than that of someone who rarely sees a writer and who is more than willing to spend an entire afternoon discoursing on the state of the world," says Hollywood journalist Lawrence Grobel.

Celebrities can be defensive, dull, and disappointing, of course. As George Martin, the producer for the Beatles, said: "If you have heroes, it's better not to meet them."

Actress Vanessa Redgrave has asked writers to sign a contract that forbids discussion of her political views and private life during the interview, and which gives her complete editorial control over any story. Like all contracts, this may have been negotiable to some extent, but clearly here is someone who is seldom happy to be interviewed.

But when writer John Davidson went on location in Texas to talk with Redgrave, the star of *The Ballad of the Sad Café*—after producer Ismail Merchant assured him that the actress would be happy to be interviewed—he observed that on the set the actress was "gracious and democratic, stopping to feed the mutts on location after meals and ignoring the company pecking order, to befriend the lowliest members of the cast."

Indeed, Vanessa Redgrave was truly charming—until faced with an actual interview. Then "she suddenly began acting like a very large, very balky teenager," reported Davidson. "She wouldn't look at me and answered questions in a way that suggested that she was only reluctantly complying with authority."

The key issue in many cases is not whether to let a subject review the text—but the reasons why. Accuracy, *si*. Vanity, *no*.

Often, clearly, it is in the writer's best interest to get back to a subject after the interview to ask for clarifications, to go over an unclear point or two. Accuracy is in everyone's best interest. Of course, make certain that your requests for clarification are clear themselves. The story is told of a reporter who, realizing he forgot to ask Cary Grant his age during an interview, followed up with a telegram: "How old Cary Grant?"

The actor cabled back: "Old Cary Grant fine. How you?"

Unfortunately, it is not uncommon for interviewees who are in demand to seek highly detailed ground rules in return for their cooperation. When *Forbes* magazine did a report on the forty top-paid entertainers in show business, the editors' first cover choice was Jack Nicholson.

"But Nicholson wanted to turn the thing into a Hollywood-contract type of negotiation: he would provide pictures, approve quotes and the text of any article," growled editor James W. Michaels in the issue—which featured Mick Jagger and Keith Richards of the Rolling Stones on the cover.

"Thanks anyway, Jack," added Michaels.

Post-interview review of materials

An interview is a terrible thing to waste, especially after it is in hand. Here are some key points to keep in mind during negotiations about any post-interview review of materials:

- Agree that the review is to be for accuracy only. For Q&A-style interviews, indeed, it may be quite beneficial to have the subject look at unedited transcripts for accuracy. Since this is usually a spontaneous conversation, a subject may use facts or figures that might be wrong. Accuracy is served by allowing a transcript check.

- Do not, however, allow gratuitous retractions. What is put on the record is on the record, and once the editing process starts, then it remains the publication's prerogative to publish it as the editors see fit.

- Agree on a deadline for manuscript review and return, so that a delay in response time doesn't jeopardize publication.

- Agree that the subject can see only those parts of the story that pertain to him—or, better still, only those direct quotes attributed to him. (And, to minimize the process of reviewing direct quotes, paraphrase to the max.)

Jonathan Kwitny of the *Wall Street Journal* once made a "deal" with a reporter from *USA Today*—"that I would talk frankly provided that if he quoted me, he would include that I still thought the *Journal* was the best paper in the country."

The day before the article was to appear, the *USA Today* reporter even called Kwitny and read him the quotes he was using, including the balancing-act statements. But . . .

"The next day, the balancing thought was missing from the article," says Kwitny.

Who's to say what happened? There's many a slip 'tween cup and lip, quoth Shakespeare. Very few interviews are intended to present a comprehensive account of someone's opinions. Rather, they are intended to get to the heart of a matter quickly—and are usually edited for relevance to the reader, not reasonableness to the source.

Other methods to secure interviews

What happens if you request an interview from a subject by mail? Some will offer generous help instantly. Some may not respond for weeks. They call it snail mail for a reason. Some you will never hear from.

Condé Nast Traveler tested 135 U.S.-based offices of foreign countries, asking each country for general information, a road map, sightseeing and transportation advice, and lodging suggestions. Three months after the mailing, the magazine was still waiting to hear from 51 bureaus.

You can also advertise for interviews. We have all seen letters in the back of literary journals or book-review sections of newspapers in which a writer announces that he is working on, say, a biography of Sylvester Stallone. The author may say something like:

> I have been commissioned to write a biography of Sylvester
> Stallone, to be published in the autumn of next year, and am keen
> to hear from anyone, inside or beyond the film industry, who has
> a consuming interest in this actor or his films.

Here is an author's query from the *Boston Globe* book-review section:

> For a book on the meaning of failure, I would like to
> interview individuals whose experiences of failure have
> contributed significantly to a richer and more meaningful life.

The author is interested in all aspects of life, including: work, progress through school, relationships and spiritual, psychological and physical well-being.

Such casting calls typically end with the author's name, e-mail address, and phone number.

On luck

Moss Hart, fabled Broadway director and bestselling author (*Act One*) once said: "To make it in this business, you need three things: talent, perseverance, and luck." (He added, "You can do it with two of those things or you can do it with three, but with one you'll never make it.")

Jeffrey Schaire, for instance, requested an interview with reclusive artist Andrew Wyeth by letter, enclosing a copy of *Art & Antiques* magazine, the publication for which Schaire worked. Six months later, a Wyeth intermediary replied that Wyeth would be willing to talk.

Knowing he had snared a tough interview, Schaire boned up on the artist's work, even recalling verses from Emily Dickinson, a Wyeth favorite, to prod his subject. The magazine that Schaire had sent Wyeth featured a cover story on "Winslow Homer's Mystery Woman."

Halfway through the 90-minute session, Wyeth said, matter-of-factly, "There's a whole vast amount of my work no one knows about. Not even my wife."

Well, now. That quiet revelation triggered a shellburst of interest in Andrew Wyeth's secret Helga collection (240 works) that was the talk of the art world. Landing the interview was "pure dumb luck," said Schaire. Yes, but in this business, you create your own luck—and the harder an interviewer works, the luckier she or he is likely to be.

David Montero, a writer for the *Ventura County* (Calif.) *Star*, grew up reading the *Peanuts* cartoon strip. He even had a *Peanuts* lunchbox. When *Peanuts* creator Charles Schulz announced his retirement (he was battling cancer), Montero got his home phone number from his girlfriend's cousin's husband, who had worked with Schulz.

After calling Schulz's office to make certain the cartoonist wasn't too ill to talk, Montero dialed the number nervously. "I had this image of him built up from my childhood," he said. "What if he turned out to be a jerk?" Montero had scores of questions ready, just in case the cartoonist was ready to talk.

Schulz was as gracious as they come. For forty-five minutes, he replied to questions on topics ranging from how his World War II experiences had built up his self-confidence to his perspective on the 1970s *Peanuts* reruns now appearing in papers (he thought his work from 1988 was better).

Four days later, Montero's story ran the day the *Star* covered Schulz's death. "It's a good lesson," said Montero's editor Tim Gallagher. "If you do get lucky, you'd better be prepared."

On persistence

Dogged persistence is a great teacher as well.

Freelancer Larry Miller called Diane Sawyer twenty-seven times for an article he was writing for *Cosmopolitan* on how to get a job in television. On the twenty-eighth call, he got through.

At the time, Sawyer's occupation was co-anchor of *The CBS Morning News*, and her workday began at 3 A.M. Miller knew that the closer she got to airtime, the busier she would get, so he would set his alarm for 3:15, giving himself a few minutes to wake up, and then would dial the newsroom.

"Diane Sawyer, please," he would say.

For twenty-six calls, Miller was screened by a news assistant. "I'm writing an article for *Cosmopolitan* that I need to talk to her about," he would explain.

He would not specify, however, the subject of the article. "Never tell the person who answers the phone what you're writing about," he suggests.

"This almost always elicits the response that someone else would be better to talk about the topic or that Ms. X doesn't want to discuss it. Sticking to just 'an article' will pique curiosity, which is precisely what you want. If you're pressed, say the subject is complex and technical and you really need to talk to Ms. X about it."

When told, each time, that Ms. Sawyer was not available, Miller asked, "What would be the most convenient time for her?"

"Well, there's no really good time, but she's usually less busy right around now."

"Okay, I'll try again tomorrow, if that's all right. I don't really mind getting up this early."

When the assistant laughed, Miller knew that she was on his side; interrupted sleep is something everyone can identify and sympathize with.

"Okay, if you want to try," she said. "Bye."

After several days of early-morning calls, the assistant took pity on Miller and told him that Sawyer sometimes hung around after the show until 10:30 or 11:00 and that he might try then. Miller did so for two weeks, sometimes twice a day when he was told that Sawyer was still in the studio.

By now he knew the news assistant rather well. Finally, on the twenty-seventh call, she said, "She is around somewhere. Let me try to get her on the phone—you've been so persistent you deserve to talk to her."

Diane Sawyer came on the line saying that she had heard Miller's name so many times, she felt as if she almost knew him. She was helpful and patient, and Larry Miller got good quotes.

"*Cosmo* ran her picture with the article," recalled Miller, "and all the effort turned out to be worth it."

CHAPTER 2

Overcoming Objections

Very few people are willing to talk to a writer unless they have a reason for doing so. You should be ready to provide one. "If people are willing to talk to you for attribution, they believe there's a quid pro quo," says veteran magazine editor and author Art Spikol.

"It's usually unspoken, most often not even implied—but nobody gives anybody anything for nothing."

Many say no because they are just too busy. The basic mindset of the hard-to-get subject is "Why should I give you my time?" To neutralize this, it is crucial that you explain what the interview is about, and what you will need from them in terms of time and preparation.

But what the subject is really concerned about is your response to an unanswered question: "What's in this for me?"

What's in it for me?

Here's where you can turn things around. No matter how much time is required, your answer to the second question is key to overcoming objections and tapping into those unspoken self-centered motivations that can empower a subject to just say yes.

"Sometimes the reason," says Spikol, "may be no more than a matter of the interviewee feeling an obligation—as though the utterance of 'no comment' were somehow tantamount to shirking one's duty as a resident of the land of the free, home of the brave. It may be a fear of what silence implies; many equate 'no comment' with guilt. It may be a naive feeling that speaking out, and thus having one's name in print, will be fun."

"Or, more likely," Spikol continues, "it may be assumed that a name in the paper, assuming it's not attached to a negative reference, will enhance a reputation or attract business."

Thus, when looking to overcome the "I'm, oh, so busy" objections of the hard-to-get subject, here is what's in it for them.

1. Visibility

> This will separate you from the crowd, Sir.

This appeals directly to the ego, raising the subject above the masses. Publicity can deliver credibility, something that cannot be purchased in the way of reputation and recognition. If a subject thinks an interview will help advance his or her image or that of a worthy cause, the answer is often yes.

Business leaders often have a strong need for social acceptance, and will respond to:

> We want to do a profile of you that tells people what you are like at the end of the workday.

There was a time when physicians and lawyers were publicity-shy. Well, physicians, anyway, often stayed in the background. But relaxed professional codes regarding advertising have made many doctors and lawyers hungry for publicity and visibility among peers.

2. Success

> This could be smart for the business, Ma'am.

Businesspersons often see themselves as too busy to cooperate with writers. Therefore, be prepared to point out positive results that may accrue to the company from the publication of the article. Tell the subject that an article may demonstrate the firm's expertise or could improve relations with other companies, that it may create a demand for the firm's products, and that the article can be distributed to customers, stockholders, and business colleagues in reprint form.

Use the same prods that PR types use when coaxing reluctant subjects to step before the microphone: "When your name is seen in print, you develop a reputation as an authority in your field."

3. Scholarship

A little pride in profession could be a good thing here, Sir.

Scholarly types are often reluctant interviewees; they do not want the censure of colleagues who view publicity as unprofessional. Moreover, there is always the risk that the "popular press" will oversimplify the story or get the facts wrong.

Richard Rhodes, on assignment to do a story for *Playboy* magazine on astronomy, found a scientist unwilling because he had seen himself misquoted after giving interviews in the past, "and had been embarrassed professionally by seeming to take credit for other people's work." Rhodes put the scholar at ease by pointing out that an interview would contribute to the dissemination of information and to the betterment of humankind. He also agreed to let the scientist review direct quotes for accuracy before publication.

"The writer's own sincere enthusiasm about the expert's discovery will entice even an introvert into showing some interest in sharing his knowledge with nonscientists," says Rhodes.

The message is often the medium for getting a source to say yes.

4. Fun

This could be an opportunity to talk about one of your favorite things, Sir.

Occasionally an interviewer can get an interview by appealing to a subject's offbeat interest. The toughest subject that *Chicago Tribune* reporter Richard Longworth ever tried to nail down was author Saul Bellow in that period just after the 1976 Nobel Prize announcement when the author was under siege and cocooned by family.

Mutual friends put in good words for Longworth, and at first Bellow promised to set a date, then he broke it and was unreachable by phone.

When Prize-giving time came, Longworth found himself in Bellow's hotel in Stockholm, where he ran into the author in the lobby. From his background reading, Longworth knew how to scratch a favorite itch of the author's.

"I explained to him that I didn't want him to sum up his philosophy of literature in one 25-word quote or to tell me what he was going to do with the money. Rather, I wanted to ask him about the artist in Chicago and the city's influence on him. I knew the topic fascinated him. This caught his fancy and he agreed to meet in the bar that night."

To Longworth's astonishment, Bellow appeared on time and with his son for moral support. "Once in flight he was polite and articulate, full of provocative ideas. The moral here, besides the need for persistence, is that many sensitive and intelligent subjects will dodge the normal interview but will agree if the questions you ask enable them to scratch a favorite itch— in Bellow's case, his lifelong affair with Chicago."

5. High Purpose

This is an opportunity to set the record right, Sir.

Take the high ground with someone who is in sympathy with an altruistic, noble journalistic purpose. Most people are willing to help, particularly if it costs relatively little in time and preparation.

Here's a chance to educate our readers.

Here's an opportunity to clarify positions or to eliminate misunderstandings.

6. Anger Management

Here's a chance to get back at those who have wronged you, Sir.

Hell hath no fury like a source who's been scorched. The checklist here includes disgruntled, overlooked, or fired employees, former spouses, or ex-friends who have fallen out.

Tommy Gioiosa, for instance, lived with baseball player Pete Rose for about five years when Rose was between marriages in Cincinnati.

"Pete's a great guy, but he has a sickness," Gioiosa told Murray Chass of the *New York Times* in a telephone interview. "That sickness is gambling. It's like an alcoholic."

Between Rose's gambling addiction and Gioiosa's indictment on five counts of cocaine trafficking, there was plenty of litigation in the air. Gioiosa was convicted in 1989. Before going to prison, however, he was approached by reps from Major League Baseball trying to gain his cooperation on the investigation of Pete Rose.

Gioiosa declined, just as he refused at his trial to talk about Rose, and he went to jail for thirty-eight months. But Pete never said thank you.

"All he had to do was thank me the day I was sentenced," Gioiosa said. "Thanks for your loyalty. I was off to prison and I couldn't believe he didn't say anything."

After balking for a year, Gioiosa agreed to an interview with *Vanity Fair* in which he talked about placing bets on baseball games for Rose when Pete managed the Cincinnati Reds, and carrying out what he said was Rose's desire to invest his money in the cocaine trade.

"That article in *Vanity Fair* is 110 percent true, everything in it," he said. "I didn't get paid for that article. I trusted the person who did it. It took a year before I did."

7. Fame

> Here's an opportunity to earn some fame, Sir.

Some subjects can be brought into the fold by pointing out that it would not be the same party without them. "Appeal to the desire for exposure," suggests Larry Miller. "Fame gives a celebrity power and profit, and fame is like money—there's no such thing as having too much."

Remember, those fifteen minutes of fame have to start somewhere.

New York magazine columnist Michael Wolff was once invited to be part of a panel at a conference with some of the greatest media minds—Rupert Murdoch, Barry Diller, Michael Bloomberg, Arthur Sulzberger, Jr., and more—with the stipulation that the conference was off the record and there would be not one scintilla of remuneration (not even a conference tote bag).

Wolff said yes, of course he would be there. Why? "Because we all crave acceptance and proximity—and what's more, do not want it to appear that we were not invited," he confessed.

8. History

> You can be part of an important story, Ma'am.

While you cannot wrestle a reluctant subject into submission, you can certainly give the wavering type some points to ponder. Tell him that an interview is a chance to get recognition and publicity, or an opportunity to tell his side of the story, to clarify misunderstandings.

Point out, too, that an interview is a chance to be an educator, to influence others who may be entering the field, and to be part of the popular history of the times. Journalism, after all, is history's first draft.

9. Salesmanship

> It will bring your book (movie, show, jams & jellies) to a larger audience, Sir.

Show-business celebrities usually agree to do interviews if they can sell something, usually themselves. It is part of the job of being a celebrity. Many hate interviews, of course, and consider publicity and promotion the hardest part of the job.

"This is the most exhausting line of work: publicity," actress Jodie Foster told writer Bruce Cook as she came into a hotel suite, tired after a day of promotional interviews. Then she settled into a spot on the sofa and started answering questions, many of them the same ones she had been answering all day.

There are exceptions, however. Bob Dylan reportedly acted up during the making of *The Traveling Wilburys* video, at one point walking off the set while "Wilburys" Tom Petty, Jeff Lynne, Roy Orbison, and George Harrison waited to resume shooting.

Afterward, an exasperated George Harrison told a London paper, "He has no qualms about taking 20 percent of the royalties, but he doesn't do interviews."

10. Flattery

You're the greatest, Sir!

While hero worshippers make poor interviewers, we do know that a little flattery can go a long way, especially with the inexperienced subject. According to a study at Texas A&M University, employees who flatter their bosses tend to receive better evaluations and move more easily up the corporate ladder.

"People tend to believe that flattery is just too transparent to be effective, but we have found that is not necessarily true," said professor of business management Gerald Ferris. "We have found a strong correlation between this type of behavior and good evaluations."

Flattery works with subjects who enjoy having their egos attended to by complimentary underlings, and with insecure types who simply need the reinforcement of consent. People who are new to a field or unsure of themselves tend to need more social reinforcement than veterans. They look at flattery as a sign that they are right.

Secure, experienced subjects, of course, may react quite differently. When author David Halberstam went to Tallahassee to interview veteran broadcaster Red Barber for his book *The Summer of '49*, he preceded his visit with a call, telling Barber how much he had enjoyed his broadcasting when he was growing up.

"It sounds like you're going to ask for something," said Barber, who had heard a few compliments in his time.

What then is the role of flattery in getting interviews? A little bit may go a long way toward obtaining a favorable response from some subjects, but flattery usually works best when the interviewer is saying something she or he really means. Even then, it should be used in moderation, lest it be perceived as a smokescreen to obscure interviewer laziness or even incompetence on the job. As the management survey indicated, many flatterers are not high performers and they use the device to cover up their shortcomings.

An experienced boss, or interview subject, can smell this. When an executive producer at ABC made the mistake of tossing a compliment at the old walrus Howard Cosell, pointing out that Howard had done a great interview with Muhammad Ali, Cosell replied, "You're a bright kid. I appreciate what you said. You can buy me lunch."

11. Sympathy

We are in this together, Ma'am!

An appeal to sympathy often works with the more experienced types. Sally Quinn of the *Washington Post* got an interview with stripper Fanne Foxe by slipping a three-page handwritten request to the Argentine Firecracker (who was involved with 65-year-old Senator Wilbur Mills) at 3 A.M. in a New York hotel.

Quinn, who was in the midst of an office romance with 53-year-old editor Ben Bradlee, told *People* magazine that she convinced Foxe to grant the interview through sheer empathy. "I poured my little heart out about the problems we both shared being in love with older men."

12. Plead bargaining

Oh, beggars can be interviewers, Sir!

The late (and legendary) Susan Forrest won a Pulitzer for stories in the *Lawrence* (Mass.) *Eagle-Tribune* that helped derail Michael Dukakis's bid for the presidency. "She was the best street reporter I ever saw," said Dan Warner, former editor of the *Eagle-Tribune*. "She loved people. She was genuine. To say she was an aggressive reporter is misleading."

Indeed, in *The Best Newspaper Writing of 1995*, Forrest described how she had gotten interviews with family members of a firebomber:

"I begged. A lot of times it works for me. It's not an act, it's just the way I am. I don't lie. I don't make things up. I begged, 'Please, open the door. Please. Please.'"

She also won exclusive interviews from many in the drama of Amy Fisher, the teenager who shot Joey Buttafuoco's wife in the head. She stood in front of Buttafuoco's house, crying in the rain, until Mary Joe invited her in for coffee. She stood in the lobby of Buttafuoco's hotel in California for three days until he invited her to breakfast.

Of course, beggars can be choosers, too. Coercion, for example, may bring an unsavory source your way when trafficking in the world of illicit behavior.

One July afternoon, Susan Forrest showed up on the doorstep of a garden apartment in New York City where a stocky local bank executive moonlighted as a pimp for Amy Fisher. She carried a tape recorder, which contained a tape of a conversation between the pimp and a prostitute in which, in lewd detail, he ordered her to perform a sexual act.

Forrest set the recorder on the stoop alongside twin speakers aimed at sidewalk passersby. She pressed the doorbell, hard. When the door opened a crack, Forrest threatened to blast the tape to the neighborhood if he wouldn't talk.

"Okay, okay," he said, "but you can't come in the house."

Then he told everything to Forrest and fellow *Newsday* reporter Jim Mulvaney.

13. Fear

Don't you want to preserve your image, Sir?

The *Saturday Evening Post* once assigned writer Mort Weisinger to do a profile of the Horn & Hardart automat, and Weisinger found that the officers would not agree to an interview. Weisinger dug into old press files in Philadelphia, interviewed a former employee who had been fired, and found that the company had a rather sleazy beginning.

Weisinger wrote a scathing first draft, which included mention of the acquisition of equipment from Germany, which was never paid for. He sent it to the chairman of H&H, saying he could document every item in the piece and that it would be used as is . . . yet, he only wanted to do a human-interest story on the long history of the automat and the affection in which it was held by people in Philadelphia and New York.

They quickly agreed to cooperate.

CHAPTER 3

The Work-Around

When you hit a roadblock, sometimes you can still tell the story—including the story of why you didn't get the interview. Robert Johnson of the *Wall Street Journal*, for example, encountered the sounds of silence while working on a story about Malcolm Cheek, a company president from Missouri who vanished during a trip to New York City. People were puzzled and unwilling to talk to the reporter.

"There are no obvious leads at Mr. Cheek's decidedly unmodest $1.7 million suburban St. Louis home, with its huge white antebellum columns and two driveways," wrote Johnson. "All the house lights were off on a recent night and no one answered a reporter's knock. A sleigh rested forlornly on the veranda awaiting a horse and riders. Repeated attempts to contact Mr. Cheek's wife, Stephanie, failed. So did efforts to locate other family members."

Sometimes this can be turned into a case of addition by subtraction. In *Martha Inc.: The Incredible Story of Martha Stewart Living Omnimedia*, author Christopher Byron tried to solve some of the riddles of his subject's storied life. Although Byron had many connections with Martha, she declined to cooperate, which he concluded was not a bad thing, since "it turns out that she is less than reliable on the subject of herself," noted the *New York Times* reporter.

He proceeded to chronicle the life and times of "the richest self-made woman in America" with numerous jaw-dropping tales of excess and success, using interviews with Martha's ex-husband, ex-friends, and ex-business partners. For such projects, "ex" marks the spot.

When *Us* magazine was relaunched by Wenner Media with Julia Roberts on the cover, the actress did not talk to *People* magazine or agree to a photo session, honoring her exclusive arrangement with *Us*. *People* countered with a "write-around," a story on how well Roberts was handling stardom, including interviews with director Garry Marshall (*Pretty Woman*) and Roberts' beau, Benjamin Brat. Moreover, *People* came out a full week before readers had a chance to see *Us* on the newsstand.

Us editor Terry McDonnell was miffed. "Wouldn't *People* have done Kathie Lee if we weren't coming out?" he said. "Isn't she their kind of gal?"

"Welcome to the big leagues," countered Carol Wallace, *People* managing editor. "We've been covering Julia Roberts for twelve years, and any time I have an opportunity to put her on the cover, I'm going to."

Interview or not. That's entertainment.

The write-around can be a risky approach, however, if a publication pretends that it has actually interviewed someone. The *National Enquirer*, for instance, ran a cover story on Clint Eastwood, flagging it as "Exclusive," as though it were something done expressly for their pages.

Inside, the story included such phrases as "Eastwood said with a chuckle," indicating that the writer and the movie star had conversed.

Turns out, the story first appeared in a British tabloid, where the source was a freelance writer who told *Enquirer* editors that the interview was taped, but he had erased the tapes. (Or perhaps the dog ate them.)

Eastwood sued, calling the story a fabrication, saying that the publication never called him to verify that the interview had indeed taken place. The court was unconvinced by the *Enquirer*'s defense, noting that the publication should have authenticated the interview, and asking the writer more about where and when the interview occurred and who arranged it.

Moreover, the court concluded, the *Enquirer* "falsely suggested to the ordinary reader of their publication—as well as those who merely glance at the headlines at the supermarket checkout counter—that Eastwood had willingly chatted with someone from the *Enquirer*." The *Enquirer* was ordered to pay $650,000 in attorneys' fees and $150,000 in damages.

For publications risking a write-around, talk isn't cheap—unless they have it on tape.

In Texas, there is a colorful saying: "Better to keep your mouth shut and seem a fool than to open it and remove all doubt." When sources don't cooperate, however, especially when they seem to be posturing or trying to hide something, you have the right—and most editors would say the responsibility—to characterize them accordingly.

Their resistance becomes a character trait (or flaw) that can enrich the telling of the tale.

And hell hath no fury like an interviewer scorned.

Maximillian Potter tried to interview John Huey for a *GQ* profile and encountered not only resistance, but a run-around. Huey, as editorial director at AOL/Time Warner, had overseen major shifts and abrupt editorial changes at the company. Potter felt he might be interested in granting an interview as a forum he could use to explain some of his moves.

Not exactly. "Three times he declined to be interviewed for this story, and even after he requested written questions, he refused to answer most of those," wrote Potter. An AOL publicist told the writer, "No one is going to talk to you . . . . Nobody. With all due respect, I don't see what the story is."

"Huey also asked his employees, including senior editors of *Time* and *Fortune*, not to speak," reported Potter. "More than 55 current and former Time Inc.-ers who have worked directly with Huey did speak, however. Most fear Huey's possible reprisals. None, however, had any trouble recognizing the unfolding drama."

When sources say no, specialists often say yes. And experts can be valuable in another way: they in turn know other experts, who can make good second-level interviews.

Closely-held family-owned companies don't usually reveal sales or profits—and such interviewees are often tight-lipped, if they will talk to you at all. But there are other sources, such as analysts, who can estimate yearly sales, and who know whether a market is growing. Analysts make excellent sources; they are usually consultants to a field, have no biased interest, and must maintain visibility. Therefore, they are pleased to talk for the record. Analysts come in a variety of forms, most often as university professors with outside specialties, or stock watchers, or banking consultants.

When the *Wall Street Journal* did a story on Victoria's Secret, the company that pioneered sexy underwear as fashion sold by mail-order, the company was downright coy and modest when it came to baring its financials in public. "The company, which is a division of Limited Inc., won't disclose numbers, but it says sales and earnings doubled last year," reported James S. Hirsch.

Then he turned the matter over to analysts and consensus observations: "Analysts estimate sales have increased to $120 million from under $30 million four years ago. As anyone who's on the mailing list can attest, there seems to be a new catalog every week—actually there are about 15 a year—but the company won't say how many millions are delivered."

The *Christian Science Monitor*'s Danna Harman tried to get an interview with Zimbabwe's president Robert Mugabe, without success. "The government basically sees the media—and whites in the media even more so—as their enemies," she reported to home base. "So, after all my requests for interviews were put off, I decided to just go over to party headquarters and hang around."

Despite the "official hate-talk about whites," onlookers were very polite. "I sat there for hours, the only white person in a 15-floor building with everyone staring at me—and really was treated well," said Harman.

"An old man tried to offer me a seat. A secretary asked me for my e-mail address so we could correspond. . . . After some time, I got chatting with the assistant of the secretary general of the war veterans who then brought me into his boss and then one thing led to another and finally I started meeting top people to interview."

Sometimes resistance can become a marketing hook. When current P&G management refused to speak with reporter Alecia Swasy, she interviewed more than 300 current and former P&G employees for her book, *Soap Opera: The Inside Story of Procter & Gamble.*

A hard-hitting write-around, it was billed as an "explosive exposé of the cutthroat nature of America's 13th largest company, written by the *Wall Street Journal* reporter it tried to silence."

There are ways, and then there are guerrilla ways.

CHAPTER 4

The Care & Handling of Sources

How to Identify & Qualify Potential Interviewees

Getting sources to say yes is one thing. Getting them to say something meaningful during an interview is quite another. And nothing is more frustrating than spending time with a source who doesn't contribute to your story.

Better to spend some time "qualifying" a source before you go to the trouble of arranging for an interview. "Qualify," in sales jargon, means to make certain that the person you are planning to spend some time with is a likely prospect for your goods or services. No sense trying to sell ice to Eskimos, goes the old saw.

Likewise, it makes no sense to spend time with someone unless the subject is likely to provide you with at least one of the two things you need to obtain from an interview: information or insight.

Some sources, for instance, are altogether too willing to be interviewed. The *New York Times* profiled one Greg Packer, identified as the "media's designated 'man on the street' for all articles ever written." Packer, a master of the sound bite, was available endlessly for reporters with questions who found this man in the street, repeatedly. He was the first in line at events, ready and willing to deliver a quotation to a needy reporter.

"My opinion is always valid, and I always have an answer for everything," this Everyman told the *Times*.

Fame has many sad suitors, often pursued by interviewers too busy using sources to realize they are being used in return. In this atmosphere, especially in the lure of television's klieg lights, hoaxsters abound. After ABC's *20/20* aired an interview with someone claiming to be Buckwheat of the *Our Gang* comedies, it was discovered that the real Buckwheat had been dead for ten years.

Another oh-so-willing source is the celebrity (often on the down side) or "spokesperson" who has been bought and paid for. A celebrity may front for a disease that a pharmaceutical company sells a particular drug to treat; the result is a sell job on the unsuspecting writer. For instance, Lynda Carter, cited as "actress, daughter of IBS sufferer" in the ads, led a campaign—including interviews and guest appearances on talk shows—to shed light on the "many women who suffer in silence from the symptoms of Irritable Bowel Syndrome." Novartis Pharmaceuticals paid for the ads, and for Lynda Carter's involvement. Interviewer, beware.

Experts' motives

In using expert sources, be careful that they don't use you. They will try. Too often, they have motives of their own in giving testimony and may be pushing a private interest or a paid-for agenda. When a Boston TV station did a news program on the Supreme Court decision on abortion and its impact on the gubernatorial election in Massachusetts, one "political analyst" was a paid political consultant for one of the candidates, criticizing the views of his client's rivals on the controversial topic.

Should a double agent excuse himself from such a flagrant conflict of interest? Should a television station have some standards and savvy in a situation like this? You would think and hope so—but it is not always the case.

Of course, experts or authorities are often interested in selling their expertise. Some are consultants to corporations and large businesses. Others are expert witnesses who get thousands of dollars for fifteen-minute appearances on the witness stand. Still others are scholars, scientists, doctors, and lawyers, and may command fat fees for their time. Why then should these experts provide information to a writer free of charge?

"So more people will know that they're experts, and so their expertise will continue to be reinforced," says veteran magazine editor and author Art Spikol. To stay in business, experts have to stay in the public eye. "Expertise, remember, is time-sensitive, and yesterday's experts are not necessarily today's. Such is the power of the press."

Analysts come in a variety of forms, sometimes as university professors with academic credentials and outside specialties. Many business-school profs, for instance, are credible stock watchers or banking consultants.

It is safe to assume that in many cases, experts will gladly talk to you because it's good for business—yours and theirs. How can you find these expert sources on short notice? Here are some of the best places to look:

Top sources for sources

- *The National Directory of Expert Witnesses* is a professional guide to over 1,500 experts and consultants in more than 400 fields and specialties. These are the specialists used by attorneys and insurance professionals—including medical, scientific, technical, and litigation experts. (Claims Providers of America, P.O. Box 395, Esparto, CA 95627; 800/735-6660; http://www.claims.com.)

- The National Press Club publishes the *Directory of News Sources*, linking reporters to sources for information. The organization's online SourceLink (http://www.usnewswire.com/links/slink.html) is an interactive resource that helps journalists locate and contact news sources in public policy, academia, government, and industry. (National Press Club's telephone is 202/662-7525. The directory can be reached by e-mail at directory@npcpress.org.)

- *The Hotel & Travel Index*, published by the Reed Travel Group, is an international phone book. Edited for travel agents, the thick tome is published quarterly and provides current information for some 45,000 hotels, motels, resorts, and lodges all over the world.

  "If something happens, I can call a hotel anywhere in the world and get people to talk to me and tell me what's happening," a veteran newscaster once observed. If you don't want to subscribe, ask a friendly travel agency to throw a recent used copy your way—and bring a wheelbarrow to pick it up.

- *The Yearbook of Experts, Authorities and Spokespersons* lists some 1,400 potential sources willing to talk to the media. They are indexed by topic and postal zip code for convenience. (Directory available from Broadcast Interview Source, 2233 Wisconsin Ave. NW., Washington DC 20007-4104; telephone: 800/955-0311.)

Experts can also be found by searching the catalog of a good library, though the material may be dated. Annual reports and business publications, for instance, can tell you who is important and informed.

When doing research on a topic, you can quickly build a hit list of experts by circling names quoted by other writers as experts. Follow this up by talking to people in business, at advertising agencies, or suppliers to the business, company, or trade you are writing about. The more people you talk to, the more names of key players you will discover for your source list.

Build a preliminary list

To save time, you want to make certain that the prospective subject has the knowledge required, is powerful enough to provide it for publication, and is conversational enough to share it with you in an interesting, quotable manner.

"Knowledge, of course, is fundamental," says newsletter editor Jim Mann. "What is the source's job? Is he close to the action? Do others consider him knowledgeable? Is there evidence of knowledge? Power is important, first because it presumes knowledge, but also because it makes things happen. Position on the power scale is especially important when probing for future developments. There is no better way to get an inkling of what tomorrow's decision may be than to speak to the person who will make that decision."

But, as Mann points out, "Every source's value is limited by the extent to which he communicates. There are people whose ability to communicate is minimal, even when willing. On the other hand, there are sources who are not only knowledgeable, but have a natural journalistic sense. They not only provide facts, but interpret them, explain the significance, point out where to dig."

When screening sources, build your list and qualify sources as you move along. Sometimes doing a few preliminary background interviews will shake loose a surprising list of qualified sources. When movie moguls Jon Peters and Peter Guber discovered that *Premiere* magazine was making inquiries about them, they were fretful that the reporters were talking only to their enemies, so they sent over a list of their "friends," who, they felt, were qualified to talk about them. (By then, of course, several names on that list had already spoken off the record in deeply unflattering terms. That's showbuzz.)

On television, very little prime-time interviewing is spontaneous. Sources are well screened for their biases in advance. By the time a source is invited to appear on a news program, someone has already anticipated what that expert is likely to say. A Washington network news producer, for instance, seeking an expert on Virginia political party realignment, phoned a university professor of government studies. To gauge the man's position, the producer suggested a reason for the realignment.

"No, I wouldn't say that," said the professor, "but Professor X would."

The producer dialed Professor X at another university and booked him for the evening news.

At most mainstream talk shows, researchers maintain lists of "experts" suitable to appear on the program. "In the case of breaking news, a researcher will flip through the Rolodex in search of academics who are Good on Television," says Janet E. Steele, a former morning-show researcher. "And even though they are often introduced as representing an outside perspective, television academics generally hold positions parallel to establishment insiders."

Over time, you can build up your own Rolodex of sources, and it becomes easier each time to call them up and get a quote or set a time to meet for a longer background interview.

Qualifying in more detail

Once you have a list of sources for a given project, and they have all agreed to be interviewed, how do you proceed? For new potential sources, study their backgrounds and check with any references or other sources who may know them to "disqualify" anyone who's not worth interviewing. Start by talking with other reporters and writers who have had contact with the subject.

Peter Nulty, of *Fortune*, learned from other journalists that Jim Manzi, chairman of Lotus Development, was as judgmental as he was brilliant—and that he liked to use the word *stupid* a lot. Such mannerisms and verbal quirks are worth knowing in advance. They get you into the proper conversational zone for the give and take of an interview, and sharpen your awareness as a listener. Sure enough, Nulty found himself tabulating the *stupids* as the conversation rolled along.

For Nancy Reagan, author William Novak did enough preliminary screening to know the former First Lady's guilty pleasure. He arrived at the White House carrying a bag of Mrs. Fields chocolate chip cookies. And when he met her at the Reagan ranch to do interviews, Novak wore jeans, which his subject was known to favor.

"Bill's like a great character actor," editor Peter Osnos told *Time* magazine. "His self-effacing quality allows his subjects their own expression. An extraordinary quality of intimacy with the person is conveyed."

Generally, when evaluating sources, a few truisms may apply. One is that good friends make lousy interviews. Acquaintances are better; there is more to learn, and the curiosity and information values are higher.

Another observation: losers in this world have to be nicer than winners. Someone on the descent may be more cooperative than someone who is at the top of his game or at least on the way up. "Nobody is better than a has-been," says Rex Reed. "They'll tell you everything. They want revenge and they'll tell you all the dirt. They have nothing to lose."

If you collect some background materials, take a careful look—at that resumé, for instance. When is a resumé too good to be true?

About 30 percent of the time, according to the corporate investigators of Barrick Security Group. Remember, anyone can manage to look good on paper. Terms like *responsible for*, *implemented*, or *supervised* are often the product of resumé-building shops. Jot down some notes for questions or topics you want to explore. Is there a logical sequence in her career path, or are there some side trips? Focus on real achievements and motivations. Note anything unusual.

Don't take a source at her or his word. As Ivana Trump's career became more and more dazzling, so did her passion for flash and exaggeration—including her resumé. During interviews, she and Donald told listeners that she was an Olympic skier, though the Czech Olympic Committee had no records to that effect. Ivana also claimed she was one of Canada's "top models," though a quick check indicated she mainly did runway work in department stores.

Another useful technique is to use the telephone to check out a source quickly and efficiently. A pre-interview call is a good way to evaluate the attitude and efficiency of the subject's office staff, if he or she has one.

Or if you talk directly to the potential interviewee, you will get a quick glimpse of the person's voice, language, and professional attitude (or lack thereof) by the way he accepts or declines the request for an interview. Is the subject flexible in arranging a time and place to meet? Does he seem outgoing and giving, or guarded and suspicious?

This is all useful information as you prepare for the interview ahead.

Friendlies and unfriendlies

As your list of qualified sources grows, arrange them in two categories—those who want to be interviewed, and those who have agreed to talk with you, but are less than enthusiastic about the project. Fabled investigative journalist Jessica Mitford, using CIA terminology, used to call them friendlies and unfriendlies.

Try the "hitchhiking" technique: use one interview to qualify other interviewees. "When you profile somebody, you can't just listen to their story without talking to the people they referenced, or talking to the people in the community about what really happened," says Jacqueline Leo, editor of *Reader's Digest*.

"In other words, it's about being proactive in every part of the story and assuming there's more to uncover at any given time. It's like being a detective," noted Leo.

A little self-serving is normal and may do no harm, but check the information carefully before using it. If you are interviewing the company president and members of the board, for instance, you might also seek out a list of key retirees and "alumni" from the company who no longer are dependent on a paycheck or company politics for their well-being.

How many will you need?

How many sources will you need? Some aesthetes and architects maintain that less is more. This is not true in the interviewing trade, however. There are many single-interview "spotlight" style stories, usually focused on the hero of the game or some specialist at work, but for general reporting, more is better. For newspaper and magazine stories, I recommend one interview for every 200 words of final copy. A carefully researched 2,000-word story will have a minimum of ten interviews with subjects, not all of whom appear in the story.

If you don't conduct enough interviews, when you sit down to do that first draft of the story you may find yourself writing on empty. Go deep. Start with the friendlies, and work your way through the list until your reporting is completed. Ernest Hemingway used to say that good writing is like looking at an iceberg—most of it is underwater. Same goes for reporting a story. Books, of course, go much deeper.

For her first unauthorized biography, *Jackie Oh!*, author Kitty Kelley conducted more than 350 interviews and took a year to write the book. For her book on Elizabeth Taylor, *The Last Star*, Kelley did more than 400 interviews and took almost three years to do the writing.

For her Sinatra book, *His Way*—based on 857 interviews in four years—Kelley went to Hoboken, New Jersey, and started ringing doorbells in the singer's old neighborhood. She interviewed residents who remembered that Sinatra's mother had been an abortionist. In order to verify the information, she went through old newspaper clippings and discovered a report of Dolly Sinatra being indicted. From there, she searched police records and found the report.

When Sinatra learned that Kelley was sleuthing his past, his attorneys filed a $2 million lawsuit against the author, attempting to stop her from interviewing his friends and associates without permission. In his complaint, Sinatra said that he had "chosen to keep private many of the private events of his life" and that he has informed his friends "that at such time as he decides is appropriate, he will set the record straight as to many such aspects of his life."

"I did not misrepresent myself. I have never said I'm doing this with the authorization of Frank Sinatra," Kelley told the Associated Press. "These stars maintain that they have the exclusive right to their own lives and that nobody else can write about them. But they became public figures, I think, the first time they hired their first press agent."

The lawsuit went nowhere, and *His Way* went on to become a bestseller, in part because Sinatra kicked up such a storm of publicity with his tactics.

Diversity

Diversity is nearly always a "plus factor" in compiling sources. Get a mix. If you interview a small group of well-educated, high-income white women and use your findings to suggest that their experience has universal meaning for women everywhere, you may have a credibility problem.

There is a constant and dangerous temptation to select sources because they are familiar and easy to reach. Some interviewers tend to overuse sources, a charge that beat reporters don't deny. "Repetition may come in quoting magazine consultants," says Patrick M. Reilly, the *Wall Street Journal's* reporter on magazines. "There are only a few of them out there with a wide knowledge of the industry."

Keep old sources in good working order, but don't overuse them in stories; instead, use them as leads for story ideas, which can be developed using other sources.

Bob Woodward is a master at this. The star investigative reporter is often seen around D.C., lunching with former cops from the old days when he was a beat reporter. They still keep him informed about who's doing what.

Big picture, little picture

Fred Friendly once observed that legendary broadcast journalist Edward R. Murrow liked to look for "the little picture"—a lonely soldier, an embattled farmer—to give us the big picture. In addition to having an eye for the telling detail, the interviewer must have a good ear for the small, the downtrodden, the person on the sidelines who may have revealing details and insights to share as a witness to events.

When writer Christopher Buckley found himself in Las Vegas to profile Frank Sinatra for *New York* magazine, he knew that Sinatra's well-established indifference toward the press would preclude any editorial fervor on the singer's part over an interview proper. "So, as the saying goes," said Buckley, "I had to work with mirrors."

His best sources proved to be a Caesars Palace security guard who had escorted Sinatra up to his room, along with a woman at the front desk, a special officer called Cisco, and Sinatra's hotel valet.

"When you're thrust into one of these peculiar situations, the best way to work is to use other peoples' eyes and voices. Like the couple from Fort Lauderdale I sat next to on opening night—she had memories of getting up one morning back in 1949 at six o'clock in order to get in line for Sinatra tickets." That, plus tickets to a few shows and notes on Sinatra in performance, was enough for Buckley to file nearly 20,000 words of observations after two weeks of work.

Tired of battling big-name stars and taciturn despots for quotes? Call a cab. Newspaper reporters often quote cabdrivers, the first people they talk to on leaving an airport or hotel to cover a story or to do an interview. Cabdrivers often have street savvy, and their names are usually printed on a license facing the passenger, so identification is no problem.

"Also, cabdrivers tend to be talkative, out of boredom or in hopes of a bigger tip," says *Boston Globe* columnist Peter Anderson.

Spy magazine did a column quoting cabbies mentioned in stories in the *New York Times*, *Harper's Magazine*, the *Moscow Times*, *The Guardian*, and numerous other outposts. "If globe-trotting reporters are to be believed, taxi drivers in other countries are perceptive geniuses whose political views are more valuable than those of, say, the country's premier."

As an example, here are a few lines from Thomas Carothers, writing in the *International Herald Tribune*: "My taxi driver . . . is an unhappy man, given to . . . recounting how much better things were under Nicolae Ceausescu and spitting when he pronounces the word 'democracy.' But he became suddenly animated at the mention of a pornographic movie. 'At last,' he exclaimed, 'something about democracy that I can enjoy!'"

In her collection of magazine essays, *Crazy Salad*, Nora Ephron tells how she was working on a story for *Esquire* on feminine deodorants, and how she knew the piece couldn't miss—because she stumbled on the small but excellent source. She was interviewing an executive and asked him how his company could be sure the product actually worked. He told her the company had "sniffers" who test it.

Ah, yes, a sniffer—the little interview with a large effect. The result is one of the craziest salad ingredients in Ephron's collection of little gems.

Working your way up

In general, the higher you go in an organization, the more likely you are to learn something in interviews—but only if you work your way up gradually. Charles Bowden, who reported in *GQ* on the culture of greed among Enron's brass, found that "The people at the top were crooks." Consequently, "At the executive level, where criminal liability exists, nobody talks. But at the middle level, where the work was done, *everyone* wants to talk."

Jeffrey Toobin, legal specialist and author of *The Run of His Life*, about the O. J. Simpson murder trial, used that approach. He got most of the facts from the second-tier sources, and then worked to confirm them as he moved up the source chain to the primary players.

Looking ahead to the next source

At the end of an interview, ask the source for the names of others you might consult. Older experts usually know each other (often there is an alumni atmosphere you can tap into), and such sources are usually flattered to be interviewed when they come so highly recommended. Here, familiarity breeds content.

Of course, before you engage in any name-dropping—one good source to another—make certain that the reaction will be positive. Author James Reston, Jr., in an effort to get an interview with John Connally, wrote to the former treasury secretary, saying, "The stories which interest me are those where the biographer and the subject have been able to forge a relationship. One such relationship that comes to mind is that between Doris Kearns and Lyndon Johnson which resulted in a very good book which was widely noticed."

Well . . . James Reston, Jr. may have been the last writer on earth to hear the rumors about LBJ's amorous passes at his biographer.

Connally was not willing.

CHAPTER 5

Backgrounding

Getting to Know Your Subjects
before the Interview

Wise interviewers would do well to consider themselves residents in Grover's Corners, the New Hampshire town immortalized by Thornton Wilder in *Our Town*. A line from that play stands as true today as it ever was: "In our town we like to know the facts about everybody."

The tales of the unprepared interviewer are far too numerous. An interview should not be a crash course in gathering basic information. Find out as much as you can in advance, so you don't drag the subject through material you can easily collect on your own. "Failure to prepare is preparing to fail," said winning basketball coach John Wooden.

A studio press agent once brought an interviewer from London to see actor Paul Newman on the set of *Butch Cassidy and the Sundance Kid*. Newman offered the visitor one of his signature Coors beers, which the writer declined. Things continued downhill from there, as chronicled by Roger Ebert in *Esquire* magazine.

"This film," the writer said. "Is it . . . ?"

"Uh, it's a Western, I guess you'd call it," said Newman.

"Is it a conventional Western, then, or would you say . . . ?"

"It's funny, now you mention it," said Newman. "The framework of a Western has been so meticulously set up that it's conceivable people won't accept *Butch Cassidy and the Sundance Kid*. That's Sundance, just like it sounds. Yeah. I mean there's enough blood in it, but it's a legend, really, and in the course of becoming a legend, the subject of the legend is remembered for great one-liners but he loses the measure of reality."

"Yes, quite," the interviewer said. "When can we look forward to seeing it?"

"That hasn't been settled," said Newman.

"These rumors persist that you're considering running for office . . . "

"I don't have the arrogance," said Newman. "And I don't have the credentials."

"Yes, quite."

"And your wife?" inquired the writer.

"She doesn't have the credentials either."

"As an actress, I mean. I mean as an actress . . . ?"

"As an actress," said Newman.

"I mean, you'll be directing her again as an actress?"

"Oh, yes," said Newman. "Now I see what you mean."

Silence.

"Well, it does seem like quite a marriage," the interviewer said, sighing.

"You bet," said Newman.

When the writer left shortly thereafter, Newman yawned and opened another can of beer. He turned to Roger Ebert, the movie critic who happened to be in Newman's dressing room during this awkward encounter. "So who made the rule an actor is a servant to his public?" said Newman.

The writer from London had come a long way to see his subject, but he expected his subject to respond to conversational prods as though they were cues from a director calling for action on the set. But he hadn't done his homework, didn't know his lines, and came off as fumbling and inept.

David J. Morrow, writing about reporters who cover the media, found that publishers were mad not because the reporting was negative (which it often was), but because interviewers seldom did their homework.

"Perhaps our biggest problem with reporters is that they don't have a good grasp of what motivates our business," said Don Kummerfeld, president of the Magazine Publishers of America. "They just don't understand it."

A strong background in business is viewed as essential for those who cover any industry. Even then, it may take several years just to learn the language of an industry, let alone to be well-versed enough to recognize and ferret out a good story. The general consensus is that beat reporters are not steeped in the past; they only want to pounce on the present. Sources complain that they are frequently called by someone who is new to the field and has, at best, a beginner's knowledge of the business. An executive at *TV Guide* recalled an interview with a columnist from the *New York Times*. "She asked me how ad rates affect our circulation," he moaned. "I was just amazed. I had to take time to explain the basics to this writer."

Interviewees like to talk to someone who isn't clueless and who seems to be on top of the news. The supreme compliment a source can pay is, "The interviewer knows what she/he is talking about."

Doing research

A good interviewer not only knows facts, but also knows where to find and check the facts. Be quick, but don't be in a frantic hurry, or accuracy is at risk.

One problem is the overwhelming abundance of information available. It is far too easy to sink into the quagmire of facts to be found at the library and on the Web. We are told that the total of all printed knowledge doubles every eight years. With thousands of publications online, searching for keywords of interest can produce vast piles of selected articles. Quickly, you can find yourself adrift in a glut of material.

Here are some suggestions for cutting through the glut, and for developing abilities to be selective and to use information resources efficiently and wisely. In general, it's advisable to prep for an interview the way you'd prep for an exam.

Getting started

First, bone up on the vocabulary. If you are interviewing a company president, are customers called clients, accounts, or just customers? Are suppliers called dealers, distributors, or manufacturers? Read industry magazines and talk to people in the field to find out, so that you can talk the talk.

Read business magazines and newsletters, and check the company's website. Learn about things like trends in the business, problems facing the industry. Use the interview to show that you have paid attention to the big picture and how this company fits in.

For personality stories, exhaustive research is the rule. One of the hottest "as told to" collaborators in publishing is William Novak, the writer behind *Iacocca: An Autobiography*, the business blockbuster that started the whole "collaborator" category (it used to be called ghostwriting). Novak knew that his access to Lee Iacocca would be limited (to less than forty hours, it turned out); therefore, he had to make the most his time with the busy subject.

"I understood that the amount of time didn't matter so much," says the writer. "It was the quality of the interview that mattered, and Iacocca always gave great interviews. One or two hours of a good interview can keep me going for a long time. Of course, I do a tremendous amount of research and voraciously read everything I can about them and around them."

For *Man of the House*, his collaboration with politician Tip O'Neill, Novak read up to ten books on each of the presidents O'Neill served with, "just so I could ask better questions and know every event he might talk about."

Clips and public records

Research or "backgrounding" a subject is like doing a little detective work. This can often be done at low or no cost. Your subject may be a nobody—say, someone catapulted from total obscurity because he lost two hundred pounds by going on a sub-sandwich diet. What's his background?

First thing to do is a "clip check." This means finding and reading what's already been written about your subject. Tap into online libraries and services that provide access to newspapers. Use the database search to get a feel of where your subject has been, what he or she has done.

When you find clips on someone, one technique is to contact the other writer/interviewers who have written those stories; they may have excellent knowledge of the person you are getting ready to interview. In the meantime, don't take everything others have published as accurate. Your challenge is to verify what has been printed, and then to find out things that have not been reported previously.

One year after the 1972 Watergate scandal, Congress passed the Freedom of Information Act to make government records more accessible to the public. With the rise of the Internet, communities and agencies are posting a wealth of public information on their websites. Surfing a city's web pages can lead you to useful background data on individuals.

At the outset, search for documents that contain basic information about the subject, such as date of birth (DOB) and current address. DOB is often an important identifier to distinguish your subject from others who might have the same name. Birth certificates are not public records in some states, but a driver's license usually is. A call to the state agency responsible will yield a driver's license with not only the DOB and address, but also a physical description. Check motor vehicle registration for the kind of vehicle(s) she or he may own. The kind of car a person drives is often an index to that person's financial standing—and personality.

If you are backgrounding a professional person (doctor, lawyer, dentist, engineer, contractor, private investigator, financial planner, stock broker, termite inspector, or any other occupation regulated by the local, state, or federal government), he or she is probably licensed. Check the status of the license to determine whether there have been any complaints or lawsuits.

State laws allow the vast majority of public documents—police logs, meeting minutes, wage information, financial documents, and many other records held by town and city governments—to be turned over to the public on request. In Massachusetts, for instance (where I am writing this book), the state defines public records as "all books, papers, maps, photos, recorded tapes, financial statements, or other documentary materials or data, regardless of physical form, made or received by an officer or employee of any agency, executive office, board, commission, bureau, division or authority of the commonwealth."

The same holds true for records of all municipal and county governments and agencies. Certain records, however, are exempt, such as personnel files, investigative reports that might prejudice law enforcement if they are released, proposals to enter into contracts, and contracts between hospitals and other health services. Record requests are made initially at the specific city and town offices. If there is no response in ten days, requesters can take their case to the secretary of state, whose staff includes lawyers whose prime responsibility is to help requesters get public information and teach city and town employees how to give it out.

Marriage licenses and divorce certificates, usually available at the county clerk's office or the state bureau of vital statistics, can yield all sorts of information. For instance, marital records available in a county registrar's office will reveal if a subject has been married before, where he was born, what kind of work he was doing at the time of his marriage(s), his mother's name, his father's name, the names of the women he married, their professions, where they were married, and who witnessed those marriages.

You can check the local courthouse and civil court files to see if your subject has sued or been sued. Why? What was the outcome? Were depositions taken in the discovery process? Are they part of the court file? Can they be obtained from the lawyers?

"If you're looking for enemies, this is a good place to find them," says Jerry Uhrhammer of the *Port Huron* (Mich.) *Times Herald*. "If the subject has been divorced, you may hit a jackpot by examining the divorce file. The grounds for divorce. The property settlement. Child custody disputes. It is not uncommon to find IRS tax returns in bitterly contested divorce actions. Watch for judgments that have not been satisfied; it could mean that the person is in serious financial trouble."

Next step could be to check with the bankruptcy court. "Has the person filed for bankruptcy, either as an individual or under a business or corporate name? Creditors can be a rich source of information."

Build a chronology

As you collect data, list events by date and build a chronology so that you end up with the story of the subject's life from start to present. Looking at a chronology allows you to frame topics for discussion during your interview. You can gain insight on how one event may be related to earlier events.

You know where to dig in and to ask questions that go beyond previous interviewers. You can also identify gaps that may exist in the story, gaps that can lead to fresh information and insights and breakthroughs in your story. Finally, a chronology allows you to see cause-and-effect relationships. This may become a fruitful topic for discussion during the interview.

Internet information and hoaxes

Use the Internet, of course, but don't let it use you. Municipal budgets, election results, census data, standardized test results, crime trends—much of this is now online. And Web surfers have immediate access to company histories, products, financial data, and much more. But company web pages tend to shine only a positive light on current issues influencing their business or organization.

Researcher, beware. Making sense of the information online requires that a writer analyze the worth of information that may be misleading and go beyond the databases to draw conclusions and write a compelling story. Sifting through Internet research is like panning a mountain of rubble to find a few nuggets of gold. The quality of the information you collect is far more important than the quantity.

Hoaxes abound. Anyone can start up a website and post false information. An erroneous Internet report that political consultant James Carville had been arrested for beating his wife, conservative commentator Mary Matalin, not only drew rebukes from the celebrated couple but also raised concerns about how sophisticated an Internet hoax can be. The false report first surfaced on the Web as a story that had supposedly originated in the *Montgomery County Ledger*, a newspaper that does not exist. The story carried a Rockville, Maryland, dateline and stated that Carville had been taken into custody by police after firing a gun into a sofa, sticking a knife into a wall, and physically abusing Matalin in the couple's home.

American Family Radio aired the story to twenty-five states before the *Washington Post* published a story on the hoax.

"I find it quite amazing even in the age of the Internet that something so outlandish could spread so quickly," said *Washington Post* media reporter Howard Kurtz. "It was a sophisticated hoax in that the person who wrote it knows how to write a basic news story."

Carville said he didn't know if the perpetrators would ever be caught, and, if so, what action might be taken. "The overwhelming lesson from this," said Professor Walter Effros of American University Law School, "is that a reputation is hard to protect online."

Two good sites that are useful for checking and debunking hoaxes are www.snopes.com and www.urbanlegends.com.

ProfNet

If you are on assignment for a story, you can dial the Internet for sources. One good service is ProfNet (http://www.profnet.com). This is an online site that relays journalists' requests to some 5,100 information officers who represent professors and researchers at colleges, corporations, think tanks, national labs, medical centers, and nonprofits. It bills itself as "the shortest distance between a journalist and a source." It can find expert sources for you, usually within a couple of days.

Lamar Graham, a senior writer at *Men's Journal*, for example, needed to interview pharmacological chemists and botanists for a story about herbal medicine. He sent a detailed e-mail query to ProfNet. One day later, he had the names of a dozen experts, including a couple of world-renowned authorities. "I consider that a pretty efficient expenditure of reporting energy," said Graham.

ProfNet is free to journalists and can be reached by e-mail, fax, or phone. Check its website for detailed instructions and advice on how to submit inquiries. Options include sending your e-mail request to ProfNet at info@profnet.com, or you can call 800/PROFNET (voice).

FedStats

A good Internet source for numbers is FedStats, which provides federal statistics on a multitude of topics. The site (http://www.fedstats.gov) is a gateway to information compiled by over one hundred federal agencies.

It offers options to search statistics by state, by topic, or by agency. It has direct links to websites of federal agencies, and also provides access to recent press releases from those sources.

Searching the Internet

"Even if you use an Internet search engine . . . to do your bidding," says Jim Cope, contributing technical editor for *Home PC* magazine, "coming up with reliable information requires more expertise than typing in keywords."

Cope calls the Internet "a gold mine of bits and bytes, but the sheer volume of data available today is unprecedented. So, too, is the potential for disaster lurking just beneath this mountain of information."

While the Internet is a good place to start research, it's important to check any source, "especially if you're going to use the information in a way that risks reputation or creates legal or financial exposure" for you or your publication. A few cautionary tips:

1. Consider the source of your source. "One of the things we do is look at where the material came from," says Margaret Porter, a reference librarian at the University of Notre Dame. "Is it an organization, institution, company? Is it an established resource? Someone's personal home page normally is not a good authority."

2. Focus on the credible. Some sources have a built-in credibility, such as the U.S. Census Bureau site (http://www.census.gov), a reliable source for social, demographic, and economic information. Professional organizations like the Special Libraries Association and periodicals such as the *New York Times* or *The Economist* also have implicit credibility.

3. Combine the Internet with traditional library resources. "Going to the physical library often may be more convenient than trying to do research from a remote site," says Jim Cope. "You'll probably get a fast Internet connection there, as well as free access to many of the commercial online databases."

   Cope recommends checking a library's website for details before you visit. You can also tap into catalogs of university libraries on the Internet. An excellent starting point is the Library of Congress catalog (http://lcweb.loc.gov/z3950), with direct links to many other libraries.

   Periodicals contain a wealth of shorter pieces on diverse subjects. The most commonly used index is the *Readers' Guide to Periodical Literature*, which indexes articles appearing in more than 150 current magazines. Updates are published twice a month, and a large annual index gathers all citations into a single volume.

   The *Education Index* cites articles that appear in journals of interest to educators. For business topics, the *Public Affairs Information Service Bulletin* or the *Business Periodicals Index* can assist in locating articles and other literature.

   Some major newspapers publish their own guides, notably the *New York Times Index* and the *Wall Street Journal Index*. In addition,

The Newspaper Index offers a guide to news stories and articles in the *Chicago Tribune*, the *Washington Post*, the *New Orleans Times Picayune*, and the *Los Angeles Times*.

4. You can use fee-based services, such as LexisNexis, which attempt to catalog nearly every periodical in print. These require subscriptions (http://www.lexis-nexis.com), which may be cost-prohibitive for those on tight budgets. "However, LexisNexis also offers some very slick Web-based services including a search tool called reQUESTer that runs from your computer and pulls information from a monumental list of printed publications and other reliable sources," adds Jim Cope. "Expect to see more fee-based Internet research resources entering the market."

Narrow your search

The main disadvantage of the Internet "is the amount of information it can provide," says Melissa Hostetler of *IndustryWeek* magazine. "When searching on a specific topic, it is often disheartening to have a search return tens of thousands of hits, or related sites." Here are some search tips:

1. Use phrases surrounded by quotes; this signals the search engine to look for that exact phrase. This can narrow your search dramatically.

2. Use several keywords, preferably nouns. Since most search engines discard verbs and articles ("the," "a"), the more nouns the better. The order of the words is important, too.

3. Check the search engine's website or initial page; most offer a button to click that takes you to a page with advance-search options and useful tips to improve your search results.

4. Try different search engines. Some (AltaVista and WebCrawler) are brute-force engines that try to catalog everything on the Web. Others (Yahoo, Lycos, Excite) sort sites into categories and can be customized for personal use. Then there are natural-language engines (Ask Jeeves) that let you phrase your query in the form of a question. Google, one of the best, combines elements of all three.

CHAPTER 6

Say for Pay

In the United States of Amarketing, everyone seems to have a price—including interview subjects. While many attribute "say for pay" to the tabloid press and to broadcasting battles for exclusives, the sad little tradition goes back to at least the sinking of the *Titanic* in 1912 when the *New York Times* paid $1,000 to the ship's wireless operator for an exclusive interview. In the 1930s, the Hearst newspaper chain paid the legal bills for the defendant in the Lindbergh baby kidnapping case to guarantee scoops during the trial. In 1975, the CBS program *60 Minutes* paid G. Gordon Liddy $15,000 for an interview.

In the wake of heavy criticism from the print media (who have a vested interest in tearing down the credibility of the broadcast sector), all three major networks have claimed that they now have guidelines that prevent such arrangements.

Some publications have paid informers and make no bones about it. Steve Coz, *National Enquirer* editor, has argued that there is no difference between "wining and dining" sources and paying for tips on former president Bill Clinton's last-minute pardons of felons.

"We just skip the dinner," said Coz.

When comedienne Roseanne Barr threatened to sue the *National Enquirer* for libel, slander and peeking in on the life of Roseanne and her then-husband Tom Arnold, the tabloid announced that Arnold was a paid informer before the couple married, and that he was sent checks for quotes about the Missus, and yes, he did cash them.

"We do have paid sources," said an *Enquirer* editor. "We make no secret of it. That's how we operate."

Pilot Henry Dempsey made national headlines when the door to his Eastern Express commuter plane popped open at 2,500 feet over the Atlantic and he was sucked out. He dangled for fifteen minutes while his co-pilot, who did not know that Dempsey was clinging to the door's rails, made an emergency landing.

But when the pilot refused to discuss his harrowing experience with the supermarket tabloids, that didn't stop the story. Both the *Star* and the *National Enquirer* ran sensational accounts of the episode, including a first-person narrative in the *Star* that carried Dempsey's byline.

The pilot sued, claiming he had been commercially exploited and placed in a false light. *Star* editor Richard Kaplan said in court papers that the quotes attributed to Dempsey were taken from interviews with Dempsey's friends and from talking to a reporter from the *Boston Herald*—owned by Rupert Murdoch, who also publishes the *Star*—who managed to get the pilot's story. The *Enquirer*, too, said its reporter spoke to friends of Dempsey's, who related what the pilot had supposedly told them.

"Still, many of the quotes fail the straight-face test and make Dempsey sound a bit like Sergeant Fury," observed Dennis Bailey in the *Columbia Journalism Review*.

The *Enquirer* story quoted Dempsey as telling a neighbor, "For ten minutes—ten minutes that were an eternity—I had stared death in the face. But I was alive. And I knew that I was the luckiest man in the world at that moment." In his lawsuit, Dempsey maintained that he never said anything like that to anybody.

He ended up settling out of court with the *Star*, but Portland federal judge Gene Carter threw out the pilot's suit against the *Enquirer*, saying that even though the facts in the story may have been fictionalized, it could not be considered "highly objectionable to a reasonable person."

Furthermore, the judge found nothing in the story that should embarrass or humiliate Dempsey, acknowledging that the coverage "bears the familiar stamp of tabloid news."

Increasingly, little, unknown sideline subjects ranging from Hollywood hairdressers to Frank Sinatra's one-time valet are talking to the press for fun and profit. *Star* gossip columnist Janet Charlton told George Wayne of *Interview* that her best sources were little support-staff types—"people who work for agents or managers, receptionists in major talent agencies, extras on sets"—and that they were all on the *Star* payroll, making between $100 and $1,000 an item.

"TV ushers make a lot of money with me, too," added Charlton. "As a matter of fact, one of my sources, an usher, made $14,000 last year."

The battle for an interview can become a bidding war, or a verbal wrestling match. *Los Angeles Times* reporters were excluded from post-trial interviews with certain jurors at the Rodney King trial because they weren't willing to pay for them.

When James Reston Jr., the legendary *Times* reporter and editor, was working on a book about former Texas Governor and Treasury Secretary John Connally, he wanted the subject's cooperation. JC wanted something else: cash up front. Reston phoned some of Connally's friends to see if they could talk about the man. "Is this an authorized or an unauthorized biography?" was the usual question. When they learned it wasn't authorized, they usually hung up. The author sent a letter to Connally explaining his project for Harper & Row. No answer.

Connally was going through bankruptcy proceedings at the time, which may have affected the negotiations. "When a man faces debts of $63 million, books are probably not much on his mind," said Reston. "I thought sooner or later he would come around." On the phone, Connally said, with no preliminaries, "I have been getting these letters from you, and there's been no discussion of a financial relationship." Reston was going to be in Houston the next week. He would call on Connally.

There, the old Texas pol listened as Reston explained the problems and impossibilities of a "financial relationship." He said the work would be tainted, compromised, and dismissed by the critics. He had been commissioned for his independent judgment, and he had to insist upon that independence.

Connally said he had always dreamed of writing his own book, and if he was going to do that, why should he give away all his best stories for free? They parted cordially.

Reston found that as he made his interviewing rounds, he quickly knew more about Connally than did many of his closest friends. His character was developing sharp dimensions, and, if Connally suddenly agreed to the ten hours of interviewing that the author originally sought, wouldn't Reston be duty-bound to let his subject challenge every potentially damaging or unflattering thing in the manuscript? Moreover, Connally had written to a score of his closest associates asking them not to see Reston if he called. Now their relationship was adversarial.

Still, toward the end, with 700 of 900 manuscript pages completed, Reston wrote to Connally. "I remain uncomfortable and disappointed about your distance," he said. "In the end, I do not feel that stance, if it holds, will be in your interest, for it would necessarily prejudice the reader against the subject." He repeated his proposal for "limited cooperation, ten hours or so of interviews, so at least the edge would be taken off the relationship."

Reston also tried to get Connally to discard his fixation with money. "A financial relationship remains impossible," he added. "I hope you will not continue to let cooperation turn on that point. This is a serious and dignified book. It will be taken seriously. It will also have a great deal to do with the way in which you are remembered. You should have a say in it."

Connally did not reply. With more relief than disappointment, Reston plunged forward to finish the book. "Had he suddenly invited me to Picosa Ranch, I am not sure that I would have gone," he said. "I would have had to go back into the book and rip it apart, as if I were remodeling a solid, old-fashioned mansion in which I had become quite comfortable."

Months went by. Then, four days before Reston's delivery date, he got a call from one of Connally's closest friends, who, with pride in his voice, announced that he had gotten Connally to agree to see his biographer. He cautioned that the discussions would have to be limited to "the facts."

"I could only mumble something about it being awfully late for this," said Reston. "I was, however, sure of my facts." Time was up. Four days later he sent the manuscript for *The Lone Star* to his publisher and left for a vacation in Europe.

Loss of credibility

Clearly, a cost of the "pay for say" approach is lost credibility. "Checkbook journalism raises the ethical hackles of some reporters and editors because it encourages the marketing of information that may not be accurate," says professor Louis Alvin Day in his book *Ethics in Media Communications: Cases & Controversies*. Like bought-and-paid-for expert witnesses at a trial, such subjects are often quite willing to tell you what they think you want to hear. Such exclusives are nearly always tainted.

Even *Newsweek* fell for one of the world's oldest hustles. The magazine confirmed that, despite a policy prohibiting such payments, it paid Oakland, Calif., prostitute Linda Kean $60 for her story of selling sex while infected with the AIDS virus. Kean later said she made up the story to get money to buy drugs.

"But the pervasiveness of the practice among TV talk shows and the tabloid media in the 1990s has certainly increased the pressure on all news organizations to conform to the economic realities of the business," says Louis Alvin Day. "In fact, many news figures now expect to be paid for their 'inside information.'" TV news needs compelling pictures. Everybody covering the Columbine High School shootings had been trying to talk at length with Nathan Dykeman, an 18-year-old who was the best friend of one of the gunmen. Only two got through: the tabloid *National Enquirer*, which paid Dykeman a reported $10,000, and *ABC News*, which acknowledged paying $16,000—not for an interview, mind you, but for a home video showing gunman Dylan Klebold, along with a music video in which Klebold acted out a violent fantasy at the high school. Of course, *ABC News* stoutly denied that it engaged in anything so loathsome as checkbook journalism. ABC said it bought this material only to bring context to the Dykeman interview, which it claimed it did not pay for.

"In other words, it paid the subject of a news story—but it did not pay the subject of a news story for an interview," said the enraged editors of watchdog publication *Editor & Publisher*. "That's their story, anyway, and we're not surprised that few people are buying it."

Competitive pressures in broadcast journalism has turned ratings wars into bidding wars for "exclusives." Tonya Harding was paid several hundred thousand dollars for a series of exclusive interviews with *Inside Edition* after she conspired to injure Olympic rival Nancy Kerrigan.

"When money transfers to the subject of an interview, that is wrong," said James Neff, a former columnist for the *Cleveland Plain Dealer* and author of several investigative books, including *Mobbed Up*. "I would never do that, and in the classes I teach, I say that is wrong."

Justifiable circumstances

When an interview means taking someone from a job, the writer might consider remuneration for services, something that might be labeled a "research fee" when expenses are turned in.

"Out of respect for 'Minnesota Marsha' and the average income she was sacrificing by talking to me," said Gail Sheehy in her study of prostitution *Hustling*, "I paid her $50 an hour. She was a working girl. I was a working journalist. Time is money, simple as that. We understood each other."

Even *Playboy* magazine, whose Q&A has been called "the command performance in American journalism," has been known to pay subjects—but only in what they call "very special cases," such as Kurt Vonnegut. "Our philosophy is when we interview a writer, we're asking the writer to donate the equivalent of his writing time in sitting down to speak to us," explained a former editor.

In this case, the payment is called an "honorarium," and only writers qualify. But what's to prevent others from responding with hands held out for an honorarium?

Athletes & interviews

Athletes who often refuse to talk to the print media will sometimes turn up on radio talk shows to discuss their personal and professional lives. First, there is a serious contrast between the hard questions from a reporter and the soft ones to be found on most radio shows.

Second, money—or its equivalent in gifts—often talks. For a promotional honorarium, an athlete who makes millions will answer a few fluffball inquiries. "As many who cover pro sports would confirm, athletes love money even more than the rest of us," observed TV columnist Jack Craig.

"In that connection, they often settle for expensive, tax-obscured gifts in lieu of cash from the stations." The stations often pay with gift certificates from restaurants or clothing stores that they promote on the air, so it costs them nothing as well.

Sports Illustrated senior writer Jack McCallum paid a visit to former ABA star Marvin ("Bad News") Barnes, an athlete whose nickname was quite befitting. Barnes had done it all: cocaine, heroin, booze, prostitutes, jail time. Now, at 47, he was still hustling. When his request to be paid for an interview was denied, he agreed to have dinner with McCallum—"on *SI*'s dollar," Marvin confirmed.

He brought along twelve friends and family members to chow down. Afterward, he asked McCallum for money—"Just forty dollars, Jack"—to take his father-in-law out for a drink. "I don't think I should do that," said McCallum. A discussion ensued.

"I gave him forty dollars," said McCallum. "Nobody ever said he wasn't charming."

When Ted Williams was turning 80, Leigh Montville visited the splendid slugger, with two cameramen and a CNN producer in tow, to conduct one of Williams' last interviews. After exactly 51 minutes, 22 seconds on tape, Williams announced: "You've got enough. Bye."

Then, as Montville packed up, the tape recorder off, Williams inquired, "This isn't a paid interview, is it? There's no money for this. Right?"

Montville said no, there wasn't.

"Well, I enjoyed it, and I'd do it again," said Williams, "but the next time there should be a little remuneration. Do you know what I mean? Remuneration. Some compensation."

"Maybe we could send you a hat," suggested Montville.

"You know where you could put that hat," Williams said. He asked Montville who his boss was. The interviewer said he had many bosses, but the biggest boss was Ted Turner.

"Well, you tell Ted Turner that Ted Ballgame would like some remuneration, okay? Tell Ted that Ted would like something he could fold and put in his pocket. You know?"

No bribe is too small. Lisa Guerrero, in her early days as a reporter at *Fox Sports Net*, pursued Shaquille O'Neal relentlessly. Although the 7-foot NBA center had announced that he was boycotting the media, Guerrero learned that one of his favorite shows was Fox's *You Gotta See This!*, so she procured taped episodes for him while making small talk with Shaq's flacks.

After games she made herself visible by stationing herself by O'Neal's locker. "Finally, as he arrived for a game against Sacramento," said Guerrero, "I sprung on him as he stepped out of his car and asked him for an interview."

Shaq shocked her with "Sure, let's do it this week."

They did a half-hour sit-down, and soon portions of it were being aired nationally. "For someone like me who's not known nationally," said Guerrero, "an interview like that helps establish name and credibility."

A good investment?

Many writers pay for interviews and consider it a good investment. Truman Capote, the highly praised author whose crime reportage changed the face of American journalism, entered into financial agreements with many of the people whose lives he chronicled in his masterful "nonfiction novel" *In Cold Blood*.

Years later, when Joseph Wambaugh was researching *The Onion Field*, his own magnum opus, he conferred with Capote and realized he would have to do the same. In fact, he used the same legal release form that Capote showed him, with some modifications. Sixty-two interview subjects were paid lump sums, according to their importance in *The Onion Field*. "Some people got a nominal payment just to make it legally binding. Others got large amounts of money," explained Wambaugh.

"It depended on how badly I needed them. A lot of the people in my book didn't get anything—peripheral characters, some of whom weren't really interviewed by me. I used other information I had and drew them in. But there were actually 62 people interviewed, and they were all paid something."

The payments began when Wambaugh realized he could not do the book without the protagonist Karl Hettinger's cooperation and permission to pursue the story. "I could not have written *The Onion Field* without him," said the author. "It would just be impossible. To draw an analogy, could Capote have written *In Cold Blood* without the complete cooperation and release of Perry Smith? That's how badly I needed this guy, if not worse. I needed him more than Capote needed Perry Smith."

So who pays? Does a publisher fund such expenses, or did all of the 62 payments come out of Wambaugh's pocket?

"You'd better believe it! This book cost me a small fortune. I had to do all sorts of things to get in to see my two killers. To get into San Quentin I had to get the one guy's lawyer and fly him up there and go with him. And I had to get the retired detective who handled this case (and was then a chief of police in Colorado) out here to California and go over the whole crime scene. I had an enormous amount of money invested in this . . . but I would have spent every cent I made on my first two books—*The New Centurions* and *The Blue Knight*—to get this story done."

Procedures

Paying for interviews is a long-standing dilemma. *Newsweek* essayist Gregg Easterbrook even argued that the practice is actually an intellectual property issue. "I don't see why professional reporters should be the only ones to profit from producing news," said Easterbrook.

"We in the press seem to think [sources] should surrender their privacy and submit to our embarrassing questions so that we can make money off it."

When a source asks to be paid for an interview, check in with the editor. Most clear-thinking subjects can be turned around if you point out that a publication's policy is no-pay, and that the interviewer is the one who does the work. The real payoff for the subject, who is being asked to donate time, is free space and other perks that usually accrue to someone being quoted as an expert and opinion leader in the story.

If that fails, occasionally the demands of a source can become part of the story. The financial maneuverings of John Connally, for instance, when biographer James Reston Jr. was trying to coax him into sitting down for an interview, became part of an intriguing profile Reston wrote for *The Washingtonian* magazine.

The tables are turned

While paying to get an interview is increasingly the custom, being paid—
i.e., bribed—by the subject to do an interview, or to sweeten the results a
bit, is less likely to occur, but has been known to happen. Geoffrey Hellman,
the legendary *New Yorker* writer, once encountered a source who wanted to
pay him for an interview.

"I know you writers don't get paid much," the subject said, "and I'd be
very glad to give you a thousand dollars, or whatever you like, for the
trouble you're taking."

At the time, the profile rate at the *New Yorker* was a thousand dollars.
Hellman reported the offer to founding editor Harold Ross, "asking
whether he would authorize me to accept it and thus let the *New Yorker*
off the hook," recalled the writer with amusement. "How rhetorical can a
question get?"

On another occasion, Hellman discovered that as he was shaking hands
goodbye with a subject for another *New Yorker* piece, the man was pressing
a bill in the palm of his hand, as though Hellman were the maitre d' at a
restaurant.

"I declined it in a kind of reflex action, which hurt his feelings and made
me feel badly also," said Hellman pensively, "as I have often wondered how
much it was."

CHAPTER 7

Just Asking

How to Prepare & Deliver the Successful Question

Interviewing is a little bit like going on a blind date. It's basically a process of getting to know someone by asking questions and getting answers. In many ways, this is something we've been doing all our lives, and it is usually a very comfortable process. "People are interesting," said John Travolta during an actor's workshop exchange. "You just have to ask the right questions." When romance is on the line, however—or when the questions become journalistic—the whole process changes.

"Questions are the heart of an interview," says journalist Penelope McMillan. "If they're good, they're triggers; if they're bad, they're silencers."

Your goal is to get subjects to tell you more than they want to—in fact, a great deal more than they mean to; and nothing is impossible for the interviewer who knows how to lure his or her game into the open with an irresistible question.

Advance planning

Plan ahead. You know what you need to get from an interview, the two *I*s: information and insight. Question accordingly. Your questions are based upon several considerations, including what an audience might expect to learn from the story.

For each interview, open a file for questions. These can often be recycled. For most topics, the answers change—but the questions remain the same over the seasons. Don't toss your good ones away.

If you have done an interview with a forest ranger, for instance, store those questions under *F* (for Forestry) in your files. Then, when that topic (or related one) calls for another interview in the future, you have a running start on the blueprint for an interview.

How many questions?

How many questions will you need? Enough to get the information you need for your story. Some interviews are quick and to the point—two or three questions may be enough. Others require scores of questions, each followed by scores of follow-up questions.

"I keep telling myself that the perfect interview is a perfect set of questions," *Life* reporter Richard Meryman once told readers. "The older I get, the more time I spend in advance on that list." Meryman did extensive research, then wrote out questions, meticulously polishing their phrasing.

Note any topics where you anticipate conflicts or drawn-out discussions. Save them for late in the interview. Start with some quick and easy topics, to get the juices flowing. Barbara Walters suggests that a reporter should "choreograph" the interview, placing more sensitive or controversial questions, which might cause the source to feel uncomfortable or slightly threatened, late in the dance. This allows the interviewer to build to them. Sometimes it is effective to alternate difficult or unexpected questions with easier, softer ones.

Writing down questions & topics to cover

It's best to write out your questions in advance, even if you don't take them out of your pocket during the interview. In doing so, you are inscribing them on your mind, and they will come forth as natural, spontaneous conversation.

Have a list of topics so that you are sure to cover everything you need. You might not even have to refer to it—but, like a net under the wire, it's there if you need it. For this, don't write out detailed questions. Instead, jot a word or two on each topic to remind you of what you want to cover.

If you have to glance at your list to be sure you are covering everything, a few keywords are easier to grasp than a lengthy question. Let the question formulate itself while you are talking. Make it conversational, not scripted.

My advice: do not write out "tough" questions in advance. Jot down key words or phrases as a reminder, but do not walk into an interview with hard-edged questions written out as though you are prejudging the interviewee. Instead, try to make the tough ones seem like spontaneous, natural inquiries that come up as a result of the give-and-take of conversation.

An interesting, useful conversation is one that moves forward, leading to a series of conclusions. A dull conversation moves in circles or jumps from subject to subject. Therefore, arrange your topics in an ascending order of interest, one that enables the conversation to grow as you add ideas and opinions in the exchange. If you enter the interview with an open mind, you will find at the end that you know more about the subject discussed than you did at the outset—and you may even have changed your viewpoint on the topic.

At the same time, be flexible. If a better story than the one you had in mind emerges during the interview, switch conversational gears and pick up on it.

Try not to worry about the next question, a process characterized by former White House press secretary Ari Fleischer as "playing intellectual chess. If I say this, they'll say that, and I'll have to counter with this, but they'll counter with that."

Better to bear down on one topic, explore it fully, then move on to the next topic.

Priming the pump

When you call to set up the phone interview, try to get into a brief conversation with your subject. This is usually necessary as you explain what you want to discuss. While working on a profile of the toughest writers in Boston, for example, I called a veteran magazine editor to set up a phone interview on the topic.

"I usually work with regulars," she explained, adding that some writers thought she was tough herself because they couldn't break into her publication's pages. "Writers have an unrealistic view of their talents," she reflected. "They don't know what you can—and can't —do journalistically."

When I called her a week later to explore the topic in depth, the first thing I said was: "You told me last week that you thought some writers have an unrealistic view of their talents. Could you tell me how you have come to that conclusion?"

We were off on a great interview because I had her full attention from word one. After all, everyone likes to listen to herself or himself. So when you open by saying, "You told me . . ." or "You once said . . ." you can be certain that you have a captive audience of one who is listening very closely to everything that follows.

Seeking the elusive anecdote

Anecdotes are little stories that add color and insight to the big story you are telling. How do you get anecdotes? Not by asking, "Got any anecdotes?"

Writer Susan Lee, working on a profile of celebrity biographer Kitty Kelley for *Mirabella* magazine, asked six friends of the writer for "a personal anecdote—something that will let readers know what Kitty is really like." The result: "These half a dozen veterans went blank." One feebly recalled that Kitty always remembered her birthday with a cake. "But last year, knowing that I was on a diet, Kitty sent balloons," she said. It was hardly the stuff of great profile pieces.

Sometimes you can give an anecdote to get one. The best approach, however, is when setting up the interview to prime your subject with a sense of what you'll be seeking. Get your subject to think in terms of time and a specific place or event. Say in advance, "I'd like to talk with you about your *experiences* in the field of widgets."

That word "experiences" will often trigger a specific story in a specific place and time. Then, in the interview itself, the "how" question can be used to get concrete details as the subject recounts those experiences. Reserve the "why" line of questioning for more abstract considerations.

Questions and how they work

If you want to know if a subject is a leader who can gather support, ask him to tell you about a time when he had to gain the cooperation of a group he had no authority over. What did he do?

If you want to know how well he can manage a complex staff, try:

> We all run into instances where two people disagree on how to do something. Can you tell me how you handled a particular disagreement that came up among people you have managed? How about between colleagues?

If you want to know about a subject's work methods and her capacity for overtime, ask her to tell you about a project she had to tackle where she had to meet a hard deadline. How did she handle the situation?

Sometimes the "when" question gets a story going. "When" takes the subject to a scene, a setting, and thence to a story.

> When did you first realize you wanted to quit the medical profession and become a tennis pro?

"When" crystallizes a specific time and place, and often a bit of scenery or dialogue will surface to bring life to the scenario.

> Well, it was a rainy June afternoon in 1999, and I was walking along this street in Altoona, and I saw . . .

The right spin

Put spin on a question. Don't ask "How long have you been in the widget business?" Instead, ask:

> Has the widget business gotten harder or easier over the years?

Such a question is more likely to spark a lively opinion rather than a flat fact. People also like best/worst comparison questions:

> What was the best year for widgets?

Plan the wording of key questions with care. Phrasing is key. For instance, when approaching a customer, booksellers know to ask, "Are you finding what you need?" rather than "May I help you?" A browsing customer will more likely accept help when asked the first question. The second question is more confrontational.

Specific words can make or break the outcome. Barbara Walters once lost an interview with pianist Vladimir Horowitz because of linguistics. "She say, 'Oh, Mr. Horowitz, I saw your concert and I must talk to you.'" moaned the maestro. "Saw my concert—not *heard*. I tell her no."

Charles Claffey once made the mistake of using the word *autodidact* in an interview with Irish novelist Edna O'Brien, causing her to grimace and say, "What an ugly word! What does it mean?"

"O'Brien was not about to let go of a good thing. Twice subsequently, at nicely spaced intervals, she mentioned The Word, looking at me as if I had proposed a toast to Margaret Thatcher at an IRA conclave."

Beware humor; avoid bluntness

Good interviewers understand the importance of being earnest. Humor in questioning can be risky. My rule of thumb: never joke with a stranger. A question delivered in a joking manner is potentially lethal unless you know the personal quirks and the political persuasion of your subject. Think of humor as a minefield. Walk, and talk, carefully.

When bad news is in the air—whether a death, a firing, a breakup, an arrest, something that is bad news for the subject—and you have to bring it up during the interview, sensitivity is required.

In October 1989, Donald Trump was meeting with three of his top executives in his Trump Tower office. When they rose to leave, one of them asked, "Are you coming down?" The three would be flying back to Atlantic City in a leased helicopter.

"You know, I'm just too busy," said Trump.

An hour later, the phone rang in Trump's office. It was a television reporter. The helicopter had gone down, killing all three executives and two pilots. "Five dead," said the reporter. "You have any comment?"

Afterward, Trump reflected: "He was a crude son of a bitch."

The best you can do is be honest, to the point, and sympathetic. Drop one line of warning to insulate the shock: "There's something upsetting that I need to tell you." Then move into the bad news.

Non-questions

One effective form of questioning is the non-question, a directive such as "Tell me, give me an example, explain how this works . . ."

> Take me through the process . . .

> Tell me what is important to you. What do you value deeply?

> Tell me about a situation when you were disappointed by a colleague or friend.

> Give me three words to describe yourself.

The question cluster

Another form is the cluster, a series of several interconnected questions. These are best delivered one at a time, in order, the next given when the first is answered. Don't deliver them all at once; this will overwhelm or result in the subject starting to answer the last question first.

> Tell me about the last time you lost your cool. What was the cause? What action did you take? What did you learn?

> Whom do you admire? Why?

The hypothetical question

The hypothetical question has entertainment value, but can produce surprising answers that may seem to come out of the blue and create a sense of unreality about the interview, which introduces an element of risk. So approach these carefully, and be prepared to field any answer with aplomb.

> What three books (records, movies, presidents) would you take with you if you were stranded on an island?

> If you were fired from your present job, what sort of work would you undertake?

> If you could live any time in history, what age would you choose?

> If you could be anyone you wanted to be today, whom would you be and what would you do?

> If someone gave you a million dollars, how would you spend it?

> If your house were afire, what would you grab on the way out?

Barbara Walters once asked Johnny Carson, "If you were recuperating in a hospital, who would you want in the bed next to you, excluding relatives?" To which the comedian replied, "The best damn doctor in the world."

During an interview in a London restaurant, actor Peter O'Toole told a reporter for *Time* that life for him had been "either a wedding or a wake." The mood seemed proper, so the interviewer asked, "Is there anything that you regret?"

"No," said the actor, pausing deliciously. "Well, sure. I'm not a French singer."

Redirect techniques

Questions can be used to take a dull interview in a different direction, though tact, imagination, and some play-acting skills are often required in the process. Here are three approaches to gaining control again, to pick up the pace, or to bring a drifting subject back to the core topic you're interested in.

Let's say Professor Snooze is discussing the invention of the widget, a topic close to his heart because he has been doing research on widgets for the past five years. You want to discuss rumors around town to the effect that his doctoral degree is fraudulent and he is the chief suspect in a series of student axe murders. While he drones on about widgetry, you prepare and then launch one of these redirects:

1. Interrupt boldly with a plea for help.

> "Oh, before I forget, Professor, my car is parked at a meter down the street. Do they ticket after five o'clock here?"
> "Gee, I don't know," [says the professor.] "I don't own a car."

Your job now is to redirect the professor and get him back on track.

> "Oh, I'll just have to take my chances with a ticket" [you say.] "Do you suppose we could look at some of the journals you kept while you were doing your doctoral research at Boremeister University?"

2. Attract attention to something more interesting on the premises.

> "Excuse me, Professor, but is that beautiful scrimshaw on your desk an original or a reproduction? I can't take my eyes off of it."
> "Oh, it's real, all right. My grandfather brought it back from a trip to Iceland many years ago."

Again, redirect.

> "It looks museum quality to me . . ."

Then, back to business:

> "I wonder if I could ask you a few questions about some recent rumors around campus before we get too far afield again."

3. Associate a new idea with the dull one.

> "Your enthusiasm for widgets reminds me of the fervor that sports fans have for their teams, Professor."
> "That sounds a bit far-fetched, I think."

Now, redirect.

> "Do you follow the basketball team, Professor?"
> "Oh, a little, I suppose."
> "As you know, several of their cheerleaders have been victims of this axe murderer who is on the loose . . . "

The cliché question

How does it feel to ask cliché questions? One of the most incessant cliché queries is, of course: *How do [or did] you feel?*

"When you interview all the time, people keep asking you about your feelings," said tennis queen Billie Jean King. "How did it feel to do this? How did it feel to do that? I want to get away from it. I want to get out of myself."

The question is not only a cliché; it is also lazy and obvious, often saying more about the interviewer's cliché thinking than the subject's ability to respond to the "feel-gooder." Stock questions invite stock replies.

Sometimes this can create a standoff for the cliché-driven interviewer. Jeff MacGregor of *Sports Illustrated* followed racing star Tony Stewart into the Saturday morning press conference in Indianapolis, where Stewart had just won the pole position for the big race the next day.

Stewart has had an incendiary relationship with the press. So the first question was, yawn, "How do you feel about winning the pole position?"

"He was supposed to say, as drivers do," says MacGregor, "that it made him feel good. Perhaps real good. Instead, he said that it didn't mean all that much, he'd won poles before, that he'd rather win the race on Sunday."

Maybe he didn't hear the question . . . ?

"A member of the press, persistent in the call-and-response nature of these weekly catechisms, reframed the question. Deviously, he was asked if maybe winning the pole didn't make him feel, say, good?"

Maybe Stewart did hear the same old question. He stood by his original, more complicated answer. Then, as MacGregor reported, "Trying to communicate his low esteem for the pole perhaps, Stewart suggested, but in a manner not so humorous as to actually be funny, that the men and women of the assembled world media could take whatever poles might come to hand and insert them, bodily one imagines, wherever and however the men and women of the assembled world media might find it convenient to do so. The press conference drew to a very quiet conclusion not long after."

Mary Ann Madden, *New York* magazine's veteran quizmeister, once conducted a competition in which readers were asked for predictable replies by an interviewee from which we might infer the question asked—a litany of cliché responses to cliché questions.

Sports figure: "It was a team effort."

Politician: "I want to give this government back to the people."

Actor (on tasteful nudity): "Only if it's really essential to the plot."

Here are some of the honorable mention responses in Mary Ann Madden's competition; they are perhaps even more telling about the cliché nature of questioning in the field of entertainment reporting (you can fill in the interviewee blanks yourself):

"Living apart has strengthened our marriage and given new meaning to our relationship."

"Exploited? Certainly not! This is a scholarship competition, not a beauty pageant. . . . I'm just proud to have been chosen to represent the women of our great state. . . ."

"Oh, man, like great, you know what I mean, man, like great probably's the only way to describe being on the charts."

Are dumb answers the direct result of dumb questions?

"Why did the chicken cross the road?" asked Ted Giannoulas (the San Diego Chicken), in an interview with *Esquire* magazine. "To get away from stupid questions."

"Maybe actors aren't dumb," actress Ellen Barkin told interviewer Philip Weiss. "Maybe writers just ask them dumb questions."

Stock questions that work

The best stock questions are human-interest questions about beliefs and behavior—questions that get to the core of a personality and her or his value system.

> What person influenced you most in life? What book?
>
> What do you do for relaxation?
>
> What was your greatest opportunity?
>
> What do you believe about people—can they be changed for better or for worse?
>
> A typical day?
>
> How do you handle disappointment?
>
> Were you a leader when you were a youngster?
>
> What taught you the most about succeeding in life?
>
> Do you have time to have a hobby?
>
> Do you have a hero?

For additional useful questions—stock and otherwise—see Chapter 22, "Best Questions," beginning on page 233.

Leading questions and prompts

Leading questions are those that make an assumption and often suggest an answer in tone, inflection, or phrasing. Dr. Phil McGraw on the *Oprah*

Winfrey Show tells us, "Eighty percent of all questions are statements in disguise." A leading question makes no such pretense—it is like a question plus half an answer.

Do leading questions work? Often, the answer is yes. "When was the last time you cried?" is a leading question that makes an assumption that some subjects might find presumptuous, even intrusive. But you can lighten it by adding a bit of spin: "When was the last time you cried at the movies?" If the subject sparks to the query, it can turn the interview into a fill-in-the-blanks segment of a game of All About Me. When was the last time you . . . thought about quitting your day job? Wore sandals? Had a run-in with the law? Took a dare?

It is also misleading and unethical to put words in a subject's mouth. Let's say you have just asked Warren Beatty, "Don't you think that chocolate is better than vanilla?"

He nods yes.

But this does not mean you can write: "I think chocolate is better than vanilla," said Warren Beatty, nodding.

Instead, you should just report the head nod. That's enough, and that's accurate. When a subject is close to expressing an idea, however, but is stammering, or perhaps inarticulate—you can use your own powers of suggestion to put words in that subject's mouth, and then quote that subject after he has borrowed your phrasing.

Here's how it works. First, it helps to make your questions colorful and provocative. This will spark the imagination of the interviewee. Suppose you are doing a story on fashion and you are interviewing a clothing salesperson at a department store. You quickly surmise that the interviewee is somewhat lackluster. Therefore, if you ask "What do you think of the unisex look?" the reply is likely to be: "Not much."

Instead, dress up the question. "Some people are saying that performers like Michael Jackson have created the unisex look," you begin. "What do you think of this whole movement. Is it here to stay, or will it fizzle out quickly?"

"I wouldn't say it's Michael Jackson," says Mr. Lackluster. "You could track it back to Elvis and sequin jackets, long hair . . . ." And so on. Quality questions often beget quality answers. Give the subject a backboard to bounce his reply off, and you may get part of your question back as a usable quote.

Another tactic is to look for opportunities to "leap in" to help a stalled answer with a comparison or colorful phrase of your own. For example, in an interview with a custom-furniture maker, a writer found the interviewee reaching for a phrase—so she interjected a colorful comparison that fostered a good quote for the finished article.

Here is the exchange:

> *Interviewer:* Is it difficult to sell pieces of furniture you have worked on so painstakingly?
>
> *Subject:* My whole rapport with the business is the actual pieces in progress. When they're done, they belong to someone else with a different lifestyle. They belong to me while they're being made, when I'm solving certain design problems. But once they're built, they slowly become disconnected from me. It's like . . . um . . .
>
> *Interviewer:* Is it sort of like having babies?
>
> *Subject:* It's a *lot* like having babies. There's an incredible postpartum depression that happens, especially after doing a show. There's this tremendous effort that goes into the show. It's exciting. You get on a roll, you build the pieces, you get everything together, get them sent down to New York, and everybody responds. Then there's afterwards, and afterwards is pretty lousy. But you get yourself together again, and you do it all over again.

Notice how that "having babies" comparison in the follow-up question sparks a lively response in the final answer. Be ready with comparisons that make any topic—whether furniture making or widget manufacturing—"user friendly" for your audience. Steer these everyday comparisons into your subject's vocabulary with your questions and follow-ups, and you will reap the rewards of lively quotes.

Even when your subject is a Mr. Lackluster.

Tighten Your Questions

When asking questions, keep them tight. Long questions can be intimidating. They can also be convoluted, confusing, and subject to misinterpretation because there is so much to absorb.

TV interviewer Charlie Rose has been known to churn dead air with interminable questions, for example. He once asked the *Washington Post's* Bob Woodward, "What'd ya think of the reporting, the political reporting of the 1992 campaign, and those very questions you raised about Clinton's draft, Clinton's married life, Clinton's sense of philosophy and who he was, and the impact of parents and family and Hope, Arkansas, on this young man?"

Somewhere in Washington, Bob Woodward is still trying to figure out that one.

If you do happen to ask a question that brings puzzlement to the face of your subject, follow up immediately. Be careful how you phrase your clarification; you don't want to risk seeming condescending. Never ask, "Did you understand that?" Instead, ask, "Did I make myself clear?"

Long-winded questions are dangerous for another reason: they invite short replies. The longer the question, generally speaking (or not), the shorter the reply.

At a press conference to promote the movie *Coming to America*, actor Eddie Murphy was asked: "Eddie, there was a sweetness and a tenderness and a poignancy about this role tonight. We know that one of the great complaints of famous people, rich people, movie stars, sports stars, royalty, is: how do I know whether she likes me for myself or who I am? Was this film based perhaps on your own experiences with the ladies?"

Murphy's response: "No."

CHAPTER 8

Asking the Tough Question

The ability to ask probing or tough questions during an interview is an essential skill. To eliminate vagueness—intentional or caused by sweeping generalities—you need to be ready to follow up with questions that call for specifics, probing for details. And by getting tough during an interview, you can use legitimate questions on important subjects to "make" news, not report it. Always listen to an answer carefully, and look for an element in each answer that requires a follow-up.

When a subject gives evasive answers like "yes and no," "occasionally," or "in some cases," use follow-up questions to pin him down. Under what conditions would he say yes? Under what conditions would he say no?

Look for hints of tension, drama, conflict, mystery, opposing forces in your interviewee's responses. And probe accordingly. There is often more interest in whatever hurdles the subject had to get over than in the string of successes that followed.

Of course, success can be an interesting topic—if the quotes are engaging. "I feel like I'm the best, but you're not going to get me to say that," said football star Jerry Rice, with just a soupçon of Yogi Berra.

On the other hand, if your subject is Mr. FullBluster, stop asking questions and shift from your inquiring mode into one of pure listening. Never intrude on someone who is self-destructing on record.

John Rocker, the baseball pitcher whose fastball was clocked at ninety-five miles per hour, spoke to a *Sports Illustrated* reporter as he zoomed through traffic, railing against Asian women drivers, complaining about riding the subway in New York City with "some queer with AIDS," and saying he didn't like the city because of the foreigners.

"How the hell did they get in this country?" he asked of all those "Asians and Koreans and Vietnamese and Russians and Spanish people."

"Why in the world does anyone think this man is worth listening to, much less worth excoriating?" asked Anna Quindlen in her *Newsweek* column.

> His career has the shelf life of a carton of milk; like most professional athletes he is one torn rotator cuff away from obscurity. The sooner the public stops behaving as though these guys are important, the sooner they will get over the notion themselves. Informed opinions? Talk to a historian. Heroes? Find an oncology nurse or a good first-grade teacher. But professional athletes? We take their words too seriously and their transgressions too lightly . . . . Athletes should be treated like everyone else. A gift of eye-hand coordination should never provide a free pass to bad behavior. . . .

Asking the tough question

Tough questions can be as difficult to ask as to answer. It's best to be simple, to be direct. You can ask anything if you act as if you ask it all the time. Ultimately, ask the tough question in the matter-of-fact manner, no matter how sensitive the topic.

When you ask a sensitive question, take note of the subject's demeanor. How the subject handles the question and prepares a response says a lot about the person. Some subjects will feign puzzlement at a tough question: "Is there a concern here that relates to the story?" Or they may tread water, trying to pull thoughts together: "I'm not sure how this question pertains to what we've been discussing. Can you elaborate?"

If the subject tosses back a question—"I don't know, what do *you* think about it?"—don't take the bait. You lose control and become the subject rather than the interrogator.

As an interviewer, you should only get tough when you think the source is being evasive and you think you can get somewhere, perhaps get an answer that the subject wasn't prepared to give.

Like Jessica Mitford, William Manchester also uses espionage terminology in dividing sources into friendlies and unfriendlies. Sometimes, surprisingly, the unfriendlies turn out to be more helpful than you expect. Manchester found that he got unexpected cooperation, even with tough questions asked of unfriendly sources, "partly because people are compulsive talkers, or because they think they can straighten you out, and mostly because if they realize that you've done your research you are going ahead anyhow."

Be cool. Don't quarrel. If the subject is quarrelsome, you could be in for what William Manchester calls "a real workout." When this occurs, "it is important to retain the professionalism of the interview. You don't quarrel. You don't introduce color words. You ask questions that are as objective and detached as possible."

If an exchange becomes heated, remain cool. Pause briefly after listening to your opponent and acknowledge the conflict of opinions. Phrasing is critical. "I respect your feelings, *but* I'd like to give you another point of view" is like throwing fuel on the verbal fire.

That word *but* escalates the issue by emphasizing the negative. Instead, try "You have strong feelings about this issue, and I respect them. *May* I give you another point of view?"

However you do it, never make it easy for the subject to take issue with the question itself. If so, it can become an alternative to answering it.

At first, Nancy Reagan tried to dodge sensitive questions from William Novak about her reliance on astrology, her feuds with White House chief of staff Donald Regan, and her troubled relations with her children.

"Now Bill, you're not going to talk about this," she protested. But then Novak would use his publisher as a prod.

"But the editors insist on these subjects," he said, moving straight ahead.

Ways to soften the impact of tough questions

Here are some ways to soften the delivery, though not the content, of the hard-hitting question.

1. Use questions that suggest you know the answer already.
And maybe much, much more:

> People are saying, Mr. Hagedorn, that your company has been dumping radioactive widgets in the Hudson . . .

2. "The devil made me do it."

> Let me play the devil's advocate, Mr. Hagedorn. Is your company responsible for those widgets they are hauling out of the Hudson?

3. Offer a little praise before pouncing.

> Mr. Hagedorn, your environmental record over the years has been upstanding. Recently, however, there have been allegations that . . .

4. Best of all, let the subject ask the tough one.
Hagedorn leans back, sighs, and says:

> This is one of the toughest jobs in the widget marketplace.

Now, hitchhike on his phrasing and bounce a question back, as though he brought it to the match:

> Yes, it is a tough job—especially when you have to deal with reports of dumped widgets in the Hudson, Mr. Hagedorn. How do you deal with that?

Sensitive Areas

The four major sensitive zones for questions are the same as the four major reasons for conflict in marriage and divorce in America: sex, money, religion, and relatives.

Often the sensitive zones overlap. Questions about sex may also be questions about money, for instance. It's income, not privacy, that often makes a source evasive. Subjects are not merely protecting their privacy; they are protecting their ability to make a living in a business that sells the image.

In his early years, gay actor Richard Chamberlain had to be careful not to slip up in interviews with fan magazines, for which he was asked "Why aren't you married?" or "Do you want children?"

"Getting married would be great," said Chamberlain, evasively, " but I'm awfully busy now."

After coming out at age sixty-eight, the actor said he wasn't afraid anymore. "I'm not a romantic leading man anymore, so I don't need to nurture that public image."

One roadway to sensitive topics is the growing-up years. The key is to offer a curious, inquisitive tone—and a checklist-like run through of sensitive topics once you have gotten into the taboo area.

Clay Aiken, the *American Idol* runner-up, spoke with Erik Hedegaard of *Rolling Stone*, who asked the singer it he could tell the story of the first ten years of his life.

"Are you kidding me?" said Aiken, laughing loudly.

"But a few moments later, he was off and telling what he had never publicly told before," wrote Hedegaard. "I can't believe I'm talking about this!" said Aiken—talking about his father, an alcoholic who abandoned him at age one. The writer moved on to other sensitive areas, observing that because Aiken was slender, with long, fluttering eyelashes, and did not have a girlfriend, "some people" thought he must be gay.

"One thing I've found of people in the public eye," Aiken replied, "either you're a womanizer or you've got to be gay. . . . I'm neither one of those. . . . I'm sure it has to do with being raised by women."

Aiken's guard was down now, and the sensitive questions flowed as though they were routine.

"So, what's your position on premarital sex?" asked the writer.

"My own personal position is that it's much more special to wait for the person who you're married to."

"Are you a virgin?"

Aiken said he watched a biography of Britney Spears on TV recently, and "she said that she regrets ever saying anything about it. So, I hate to repeat myself, but: I think it's much more special to wait for the person who you're married to."

"Masturbation?"

"Are you kidding me? I hope that's a question and not a proposition! Anyway, I don't think it makes you go blind."

"And you know that from personal experience?"

"You stop right now!"

"Breakfast cereal?"

"Cinnamon Toast Crunch!" said Aiken, with relief in his voice.

At *Glamour* magazine, where the subject is all sex all the time, there is a constant search for subjects who will spill all. Month after month, people reveal their most intimate relationship secrets in the magazine to an audience of nearly 13 million total strangers.

"It's not easy," says an editor behind the scenes. "The first step is to scout out interview subjects who will agree to dish about their own love lives with our note-taking reporters."

Working with sources close to home is a great way to start. "We start by grilling our friends, and then our friends' friends," says *Glamour* contributor Lesley Dormen. "I think of them as my anecdote Mafia—a core group of wildly articulate people who have tons of tales they're willing to tell."

Not all interview subjects are friends of the writers, of course. Many are subjects the magazine finds through stringers—a team of reporters across the country—or even through queries over the Internet. Once these subjects agree to be interviewed, of course, the intimacy just begins.

"You can't just ask deeply personal questions point-blank," says Dormen. "You have to enter into a dialogue, and that often means revealing some of your own secrets to the person you're interviewing.

"Of course, women are more comfortable with these conversations than men." How so? Well, men will talk candidly about sex and love, according to columnist Glen Freyer, who wrote "Glamour Asks: Men Answer," but only under certain conditions.

"If you ask a relationship question of more than one guy at a time, it's the kiss of death—all you'll get are jokes," said Freyer. "But if you talk to guys one-on-one and ask questions with a straight face as if it really matters, they'll spill their guts."

Watch for stalling techniques

When you ask a sensitive question, watch out for any of several "stalling" techniques that subjects may try to use while thinking of an appropriate response. Remember, often they've been coached in the gentle art of deflecting questions they consider tricky.

"What do you do when an interviewer throws you a curve?" writes advertising manager Lin Grensing in the pages of *The Toastmaster*, a publication for executives trying to learn how to think on their feet. "You can use several 'stalling' techniques while you think of an appropriate response. A statement such as 'That's an interesting question' can do the trick."

Morley Safer, after establishing on *60 Minutes* that Arthur Fiedler was a firehouse buff, asked the 83-year-old maestro, "Up in heaven, would you choose the company of firemen or the company of musicians?"

"Well, that's quite a question," replied Fiedler as the camera moved in for a close-up of his sense of dismay. He didn't answer it.

Other evasion tactics that Grensing calls the "best way to answer any question that makes you feel uncomfortable or takes you off guard" are the following responses:

> I'm sorry but I can't address that issue.

> I'm not at liberty to comment on that.

> I'm not sure what you're getting at. Could you rephrase the question?

> I'm sorry, but I'm not in a position to answer that question.

Simple follow-ups like "Why?" can lead to a merry chase and eventual capture. If a subject says "no comment," point out that "no comment" can make a subject look like a Mafia suspect appearing before a congressional committee. In many instances, "no comment" is a knowing comment.

"I resent when I read in the paper I was unavailable for comment," University of Kentucky athletic director Cliff Hagan once explained. "I'm always available for comment, even if my comment is 'No comment.'"

Of course, the evasive action of an experienced subject trying to avoid saying "no comment" can make for some lively wiggling. Governor George Deukmejian of California was once quoted in the *Los Angeles Times* as responding to a question this way: "Well, I don't think that you should interpret my not taking a position on it at this time as a determination to do anything on it at the moment, but, in the event that I don't take a position on it during the next three weeks, I think you'll be able to reach a conclusion."

How's that?

Author Roger Kahn conducted an interview with Ron Blomberg, an often-injured and -maligned Yankee player who was on the mend from a shattered knee and who wanted to chatter to anyone who cared, because Yankee ownership seemed indifferent. "Was the manager sympathetic, Ron?" asked Kahn.

"Billy Martin is a good manager," said Blomberg. "He gets a team winning."

"What do you think of Billy Martin as a person?" asked Kahn.

The writer noticed that Blomberg's eyes flared and he set his jaw.

Kahn wrote: "'I have no comment on Martin as a person,' Blomberg said, commenting on Martin as a person."

Point out, too, that as an interviewer you are accountable to the public. So are many of the people you interview, even though they may think otherwise. Many PR types do not always like to pay attention to getting out the full story and pay little attention to any standard of candor for the public interest. Consider the high-handed attitude of Mobil's legendary in-your-face Herb Schmertz, who has been called the Billy Martin of corporate PR.

"Often, when reporters approach you for an interview, they will imply that you have no real choice in the matter," he says in his guerrilla manual for corporate executives, *Good-Bye to the Low Profile* (with the ubiquitous William Novak). "They may say or suggest that if you don't cooperate, you'll be violating some unwritten law, or that your non-cooperation will make you look bad. Don't fall for any of this. Always talk to the press because you want to, or because it will be good for you or your institution. But never do so because you have to."

Toughness & gender

The majority of journalism school graduates today are women. As women journalists move into other newspaper departments, the segregated "women's sections" of newspapers are disappearing. Are there differences in style?

Kay Mills, author of *A Place in the News: From the Women's Pages to the Front Page*, believes that women think differently from men. "Women are less afraid to ask fundamental questions such as, 'What do you do in a day?'"

Which is not to say that women are better reporters than men, according to Mills. "It's not a question of good or bad, but of seeing the world a little differently. Women know better what other women want to read."

Women have both advantages and disadvantages when it comes to getting tough. Women often face a double standard. Kitty Kelley—a writer whom one observer called "the literary equivalent of a serial killer"—knows that her job as an unauthorized biographer is to turn up dirt. One cannot expect the subjects of her exposés—Jackie Onassis, Elizabeth Taylor, Frank Sinatra, and Nancy Reagan—or their fans to like her, because her type of journalism demands a certain talent for rudeness.

Yet, "what is seen as intrepid and curious in male investigative reporters is called shameless and pushy in female investigative reporters," observes Susan Lee in a Kelley profile for *Mirabella* magazine.

Women interviewers on the job may face antagonism from men who perceive them as privacy invaders. When Kelley proposed doing her biography of Frank Sinatra, for instance, she went to New York to talk to her publisher about a subject she considered the ultimate challenge, one that other investigative reporters had avoided. The publisher asked, "Why should we get a girl to do this when the guys won't?"

"Because they don't have the balls," said Kelley.

On the other hand, males who still believe in chauvinism may find themselves easy targets for those who know how to push those button effectively. Journalist Lillian Ross used her wiles to tag along with Ernest Hemingway during one of the novelist's visits to Manhattan, where he nearly forgot that she was around. When the devastating *New Yorker* profile appeared, Ross had managed to capture his every swagger, every speech inflection, and to draw a picture of a man who was a few degrees off course by most standards.

Journalist Linda Witt once spent more than a year trying to get an interview with Chicago's Mayor Richard J. Daley, finally penetrating his inner circle by talking with consumer sales commissioner Jane Byrne, who called the mayor, who thought it was a great idea.

Witt was told that there were no preconditions on the interview, but that she would only have fifteen minutes. "He was incapable of being mean to a woman," recalled Witt afterward. "It was a tremendous interview. I talked with him for an hour and 45 minutes."

Toughness & stamina

Finally, if you anticipate asking tough questions during a tough interview, be ready for it physically. If you have to see several people in the course of a day, it would probably be best to do the tough work in the morning, before interview fatigue settles in.

"I'm definitely not tough," says writer Peter Nulty, who spent three months hanging out with and interviewing the toughest bosses in America for *Fortune* magazine. His editors would disagree, of course, and certainly the magazine's reputation for doing tough reporting paved the way.

In fact, a reputation for toughness can be a good thing for business. Nulty found that some of the toughest bosses in America came on like pussycats in person. Many confessed they were afraid of journalists, and one tough company chairman even called out to Nulty as he left his office:

"When you sit down to write, think of my mother—she's 80!"

CHAPTER 9

The Well-Tempered Interview

Managing the Flow of the Session

Somewhere it is written that if you want to make God laugh, just tell Him (or Her) your plans. Interviewers have known this for a long time; their best-made plans have been creating lots of heavenly chortles over the years. No matter how much planning you have done, once underway an interview is not likely to be as organized as you would prefer.

Most interviews simply unfold. Josh Resnek of *The Improper Bostonian* showed up to interview Leslie Abramson in a Boston hotel suite as the feisty defense attorney—half-dressed, rolling curlers in her hair—was getting ready to do a television tour promoting her biography. "You can write anything you want," said Abramson, "but I don't want you writing about my hair."

She lit a cigarette. "You don't mind if I smoke, I trust," she said. "Interviewers seem to be more interested in my hairstyle than what I have to say," she added, studying herself in the mirror of the vanity.

She pulled and tugged at said hair, until it was the curly, blown-out, ultra-teased coif that became familiar to television viewers across the nation when she was *Nightline*'s commentator during the seemingly endless O. J. criminal trial. Finally, she was finished with her hair.

"Now, you'll excuse me," she said with a smile. "I've got to get dressed." Abramson was in a meshy bra top and slacks when this interview began, somewhat distracting, but obviously of no concern to the fiery barrister, who stands about five feet tall without her shoes, which she didn't have on her feet yet.

Resnek took it all in.

Before you go into the room

Meeting your subject face-to-face is like going on a blind date. Anticipate anything. If you are driving, bring change for the parking meter. Always be prepared for a canceled appointment, or for showing up and finding no one there. Slips happen. Plan ahead thoroughly, but try to remain flexible. And be prepared to capitalize on surprise opportunities to take the interview in an unexpected direction.

Jitters are normal for most interviewers. Miles Davis: "If you ain't nervous, you're not paying attention." In fact, a bit of stage fright can empower a performance. So inhale deeply and hold your breath long enough to feel the stress. Then let it out and work yourself slowly into a deeply relaxed mental state.

Before going in, think through your strategies, step by step, leading to a successful outcome. "Imagination is the beginning of creation," said George Bernard Shaw. "You imagine what you desire, you will what you imagine, and at last, you create what you will." Mental rehearsal, the act of envisioning specifically what you will do in a certain situation, is a technique used by athletes to envision success. Golfers do this on the putting green; they study the shot and envision the ball rolling into the cup as they get ready to use their trusty putter. Seeing is believing, and believing is the beginning of any achievement.

Script in your mind what you will say, points you will cover, key questions you will ask, and responses you will make. Most of all, visualize the achievement of your goal: a great interview that will make your story come to life.

To relax, try the Sarnoff squeeze. Dorothy Sarnoff, chairperson of Speech Dynamics in New York, has assisted even veteran speakers who find themselves with weak knees, sweaty palms, and a shaky voice. To combat the jitters, Sarnoff suggests that just before going into the room, sit up, lean forward slightly and place your palms together at the base of your ribs, fingers pointing up. Then contract your muscles just below the ribs while exhaling slowly. Explains Sarnoff: "The squeeze helps calm the nervous system."

Internally, cheer yourself on. And don't sweat the small stuff. This is no time for perfectionism. Napoleon Hill: "No great enterprise will ever begin if all obstacles·must first be overcome."

You are often dealing with subjects who are likely to be as nervous in your presence as you are in theirs. After all, you will have the final word. If fear of public speaking is the worst fear of all . . . can being interviewed be very far behind?

Adweek did a Q&A with Dennis Ryan, a wunderkind creative director at agencies where he directed ads featuring megastars such as Michael Jackson. Ryan was comfortable in the land of creative giants. Up close and personal, however, he was jittery. When asked, "What's your biggest fear?" he spoke for countless other apprehensive subjects when he replied: "Sounding like a self-righteous dork in this interview."

First impressions: be relaxed and confident

Try to check out the environment in advance. At least get a description of the office from the receptionist. Call and ask if there is an electrical outlet for your recorder, and strike up a conversation on the setting so that you don't feel isolated from the scene and stressed at the feeling of being a stranger in a strange land.

Remember that the interview starts the moment you step in the front door. Is there a guard? A receptionist? A personal assistant or secretary? They are all aware of your actions and reactions.

There is the old adage that "the handshake is everything." If you are weak- or moist-wristed, you should practice your handshake before proffering it to a subject who may be put off by anything less than a stout squeeze. Remember, as in job interviews, agreeableness often trumps competence.

Malcolm Gladwell, author of the bestseller *The Tipping Point*, analyzed the impressions one gives (and gets) during job interviews. These are similar to journalistic interviews in that the subject sits down with a perfect stranger for an hour or so and attempts to draw conclusions about that stranger's intelligence and personality.

"But what, exactly, can you know about a stranger after sitting down and talking with him for an hour?" asks Gladwell in a story for the *New Yorker*. "When we make a snap judgment, it really is made in a snap. It's also, very clearly, a judgment: we get a feeling that we have no difficulty articulating."

Gladwell spent some time with Nalini Ambady, an experimental psychologist at Harvard University who conducted experiments to determine the validity of snap judgments. Using videotapes of teaching fellows, she presented observers with a ten-second silent video and a fifteen-item checklist of personality traits for rating the teachers.

"In fact, when Ambady cut the clips back to five seconds, the ratings were the same," reported Gladwell. "They were even the same when she showed her raters just two seconds of videotape. That sounds unbelievable unless you actually watch Ambady's teacher clips, as I did, and realize that the eight seconds that distinguish the longest clips from the shortest are superfluous; anything beyond the first flash of insight is unnecessary."

Next, Ambady compared those snap judgments of teacher effectiveness with evaluations made, after a full semester of classes, by students of the same teachers. The correlation was "astoundingly high," says Gladwell. "A person watching a two-second silent video clip of a teacher he has never met will reach conclusions about how good that teacher is that are very similar to those of a student who sits in the teacher's class for an entire semester."

Clothes

Clothes make an interviewer's first impression. It is probably best to wear something that seems effortless; something the subject will be able to relax with.

In general, conservative clothing is best. Interviewees don't like to be intimidated by someone who looks like a fashion model. Seek the advice of experts, people who can lead you to the kind of appearance that is always becoming for you and is likely to be appropriate for the particular interview you are doing. Your "fashion statement" can instantly instill confidence in the interviewee, so it pays to have a varied repertoire of "looks" if your job puts you in contact with many types of subjects.

For instance, if you dress like a *GQ* model to interview a Green Peace environmentalist, you might not get that subject to confide in you. Save the Armani for interviewing a successful retailer. Conversely, the sweater and chinos ensemble you used for the environmentalist interview might make an attorney or bank executive quite uneasy.

For a basic look, image consultants recommend a conservative jacket for women, a jacket for men. For men, suits (when appropriate) should be of natural fabrics, dark blue or dark gray for most business settings; shirts—white or a very light blue. For accessories, consider black laced shoes, black socks, dark tie with a conservative stripe or pattern. Watch out for brown or green polyester suits, or shirts with exotic stripes.

For women: according to Deborah Tannen, author of *Talking from 9 to 5* (about men's and women's conversational styles), every decision a woman makes about her appearance is symbolic and significant.

She describes the "standard TV dress for women," for instance. "When I appear on television, I always wear a red, standard-cut jacket, a black turtleneck, one piece of jewelry, and large but rather plain earrings," she told interviewer D. C. Denison for the *Boston Globe Magazine*. "You don't want to distract from what you're saying, which is a huge problem for women."

For both men and women, looking good is important on almost every job. In an online marketing research survey conducted by Bernice Kanner and American Dialogue (reported on in *Advertising Age*), the majority of respondents said they discriminate against others based on looks. Indeed, vanity is probably the least venomous of the seven deadly sins. Given a choice between a polyester outfit that they would have to wear at least twice a week or a pronounced "New Yawk" accent, 75 percent said they would opt for the irritating voice.

When sizing up a member of the opposite sex, one-third said the smile was the most important feature. After that, 26 percent said the eyes, 15 percent the body, 4 percent the hair, and only 1 percent focused on the legs.

Notably, 90 percent think that good-looking people fare better in the workplace. And 96 percent said that overweight people are discriminated against.

Some 48 percent said they had been discriminated against because of the way they look, and 57 percent admitted to discriminating against someone else for looks.

So how should an interviewer look? In a word: good.

Openers

Most interviews are easygoing exchanges. The standard advice is to open on an easy note. You might express thanks, perhaps.

> I appreciate your finding time to visit with me.

Then open with some easy questions. These help establish trust and take the butterflies out of an encounter. For you as interviewer, there is bound to be some strain at the outset. After all, you are using questions to get information and quotes from someone for a story you have to produce. If the questions are interesting enough, however, the source begins to enjoy the process, and you will too.

Certainly, the depth and drama of the interviewee's answers will depend heavily on what he or she thinks of your questions. "Judge a man by his questions rather than by his answers," says Voltaire.

Titles & names

You don't need to address your subject by name in every sentence, but if the interviewee has a professional degree, get the title right. "Is it Dr. Merman, or should I call you Madam?" Little expressions of interest, approval, or curiosity are good prods to keep the conversation moving along.

Don't try to be instantly familiar. He may be David to millions of viewers, but to you, on an interview, he is Mr. Letterman, unless you have his permission to address him by his first name.

Getting the ball rolling

To diffuse the artificiality, the late workshop director Tom Hunter used to advocate two basic goals. "First, work on yourself to build a real sense of interest, either in the person or the subject matter.

"Second, move the interview to a level of real conversation, as quickly and closely as possible. That's one reason why small talk is a good way to open the interview. It sets the conversational tone."

Consider yourself a gracious host, not a guest. (A guest will wait to be introduced; a host introduces himself.) Remember, you are being studied, observed, and evaluated.

Body language & eye contact

Some interviewers use body language to help get a favorable response—constant eye contact, appearing relaxed, leaning toward and possibly even touching the subject. A little touching can go a long way as an indicator of trust, even superficial intimacy.

How long can you touch? Well, a study by the School of Hotel Administration at Cornell University found that even a "prolonged" touch—of as many as four seconds—by a restaurant server does not provoke a negative reaction in a patron, confirming other research that a touch can help when putting the touch on someone for a tip.

In most cases, eye contact signifies respect. At meetings, whom does the speaker look at the most when speaking? Probably the person he or she most respects.

Actress Kathleen Turner once expounded on the importance of eye contact, and how it can create an aura that is most beneficial. "I've learned to use my eyes to focus attention," she explained. "And I'm real good at concentrating. What people show you by their eyes, their interest, is what's beautiful. It's like showing somebody you're having a good time."

But the eyes don't always have it. Some subjects wear dark glasses, for one thing. Also, be mindful that there can be differences in body-language attitudes and responses based on cultural upbringing, economic class, or ethnic heritage.

A team of Boston University psychologists analyzed films for eye contact and direction of gaze. They determined that a white subject tends to look away from the person he is talking to and to look toward someone he is listening to. African Americans tend to do the opposite.

Therefore, if an Anglo-American interviewer glances at a black subject, he may think he has lost his subject's attention because the interviewee is looking off into the distance. "Why don't you look at me when I'm speaking to you?" would be an inappropriate attitude here. A black interviewer, meanwhile, may encounter such strong eye contact while asking questions that there could be a feeling of scrutiny and critical inspection.

Psychologists have also determined that females engage the eyes of their subjects more often than do males. One study found that male interviewers obtain fewer responses than females, and fewest of all from fellow males—while female interviewers obtain their highest responses from men, except for young women talking to young men, when there may be more going on than an exchange of information.

Sometimes too much eye contact can be overbearing and subject to misinterpretation. After all, this is an interview we are trying to develop, not a relationship. Often, after asking a question—"Mr. Hagedorn, what publications do you read to help you keep abreast of what's going on in the business?"—it is best to put your head down and prepare to take notes. This can actually have a relaxing effect on the subject, and open him up to the question. Now he is ready to hold forth.

A poker face?

Athletes talk of having a "game face," which means taking care of business, no fooling around—the demeanor that some interviewers bring to the task. Roger Ailes, in his book *You Are the Message*, cautions against using too much of a poker face on the job. Some interviewers believe that in maintaining a poker face, regardless of the emotional state they are in, they achieve a strategic advantage. Ailes says the opposite is true, and that credibility comes when your audience feels you are completely open and not hiding anything from them.

Thomas Murray, a magazine bureau chief, says it took him a "good many years" before he felt secure enough to drop the stone-faced façade of the professional journalist who's heard it all before. "No matter what people told me, I just took it all down and didn't react," he explained.

"But once I got past that and began to react and respond, it completely changed the quality of my interviews and the quality of the quotes I was able to get out of people."

"When all you're after is surface information, it doesn't much matter," observed business writer and writing coach Tom Hunter. "It's all aboveboard, you both know what you're after—basic facts. You go in, you get them, and you leave."

It's much different, however, for the in-depth interview, where it's not just surface scratchings. "You're trying to get to the bottom of things; probing for good, quotable quotes," added Hunter, "or desperately searching for something that could bring an otherwise dreary story alive."

In these situations, one of the worst things is to treat the subject as nothing more than a source, someone from whom you are going to extract whatever you need as quickly as possible, and then you're out of there. Instead, be aware of your role, not only as an interviewer, but also as an audience.

"How you react and respond to other people and what they're telling you is going to greatly influence what you're able to come away with," added Hunter. "It's the same as in the theater. When the audience is sitting back on its hands, it drags down the performance on the stage. But when the audience is up on the edges of its seats, the cast wants to give so much more because it's getting such positive feedback."

Be open-minded

Often, when setting up an interview, the subject will ask, "What's the slant on this story?" Don't answer that, even if the story is starting to develop one. Determining the slant of the story is like navigating a boat in uncertain weather. You begin by collecting data from many sources to draw a general assumption, but must be quick to respond and adapt when new information comes along.

Be open to the story you *aren't* looking for. When unexpected patterns occur, act on them. The story may take you in another, more rewarding direction.

"Interviewers are like actors," Warren Beatty once told Lawrence Grobel as they sat on the patio of his penthouse apartment in Hollywood. "An interviewer can ask you a cliché question, but you can tell what he's capable of hearing or what he's really searching for by his inflections. You can almost tell what someone intends to do to you by his face, his body type or his body language."

Then he added a final touch of cynicism: "Most interviewers have their story written when they show up, and they want you to do something to prove they're right or to fill it in for them."

Gaining trust & empathy through self-revelation

Norman Mailer said that he felt exploited the moment he stepped into an interview. Interviewers, he explained, serve up 1 percent of themselves in the questions they ask, but the subjects who answer have to give back 99 percent.

"To ease this feeling, tell a little something about yourself to the people you interview," advised Tom Hunter. "You'll also find it's one of the most effective ways to draw people out."

Nan Robertson, author and veteran *New York Times* reporter, for instance, found that if she revealed something in her own life that spoke to the people she was interviewing, they would open up to her.

"This is something I came to only after many years as a newspaper reporter," she said.

Robertson once interviewed two actresses who played in *'night, Mother*, a two-character play by Marsha Norman about a young woman who announces to her mother at the beginning of the evening that she intends to commit suicide that very evening. "Well, I got talking with these two actresses about it," said Robertson. "And I asked them if they had ever contemplated suicide or if they had ever been depressed.

"And then I said, 'because *I* have. I have been clinically depressed, and I have been hospitalized for depression, and I have contemplated suicide.' This just absolutely opened them up. And both actresses had suffered depression, had contemplated—repeatedly contemplated—suicide because of things that had been happening in their private lives."

Is this play-acting on the part of the interviewer? No, "this was something more than a technique," said Robertson. "It was saying to somebody, 'I trust you, and I will tell you this private thing about myself.' And they did trust me. They just opened up, and they told me all these extremely sensitive and private things—not for off the record—but really because it had moved them to know that I was not some hot-shot reporter who was sitting down with them but that I was a human being who had suffered and who had contemplated this ghastly act, although I had never attempted it.

"I had opened up myself, and I got something back from them in return. And I don't mean that in any selfish way. They gave to me because I gave to them."

"Here it was a natural question for Nan Robertson to ask, because of the nature of the play," observed Hunter. He turned this lesson into something much more subdued, even routine, for interviews that had less emotional residue. When a doctor, for instance, told Hunter she had wanted to be in medicine from the time she was eight years old, Hunter came back with, "Aren't you lucky. I was in my twenties before I knew what I wanted to do."

The link was established.

If the head of a large organization was the subject, Hunter would ask, "How do you stay on top of all the things you have to stay on top of? I'd never be able to do that."

Remember that you are looking for opportunities for self-revelation in every interview. They exist, but you have to be on the alert to use them— and to evaluate, on the spot, how effective a particular moment can be in helping you to connect with the subject and draw him or her out.

Other behavior tips

If an interview occurs over lunch or dinner, don't get too comfortable and let your guard down. Don't drink hard liquor at meals. Don't order messy food. Don't joke with restaurant personnel or complain about anything. Don't let the subject reach for the check.

Bellying up to the bar and drinking on the job are not recommended for interviewers, but it may be necessary to work your way into the schedule of hard-drinking sources. For the famous cover story *Time* magazine did on Ernest Hemingway in 1955, senior editor Robert Manning called the author in Cuba from his home in New York and talked to him for an hour and a half, trying to prevail on the novelist to let him come down for an interview. Hemingway had just survived a plane crash in Africa, where he had come out of the jungle with a bunch of bananas in one hand and a bottle of gin in the other.

Robert Manning knew that the author could be warm and generous and friendly—if he liked you. He had also done enough homework to know that he should not bring up the topic of Hemingway's father's suicide; and he had the good sense to bring along a bottle of 30-year-old Ballantine Scotch.

When Hemingway asked if he'd like a drink, and Manning replied, "God, I'd love a Martini," the rapport was off and running. "Good," said a relieved Hemingway. "I don't trust anyone who doesn't drink." The fact that Manning had some experience in fishing helped, too. In all, the reporter spent three and a half "great days with Hemingway, fishing and staying up late and talking about everything—Joyce, Eliot, Pound, drinking, even his father's suicide." That last was a topic that Hemingway brought up himself. Manning asked if he thought it took courage to commit suicide.

"No," said Hemingway, "I think there's a lot of egotism in it."

As Manning reflected to fellow journalist Dan Wakefield recently, "That came back to me years later when he committed suicide himself."

Victor Merina, a writer at the *Los Angeles Times* for nearly twenty years, found himself working on a magazine story in the Philippines, where he not only had to drink beer to gain access to sources; he also had to consume *balut*, a Philippine delicacy consisting of boiled embryonic duck egg, which features a crunchy duck embryo complete with premature feathers.

"I was in Manila sitting with several reluctant sources who were eyeing me—a reporter born in the Philippines but raised in America—with some suspicion," said Merina. "Before answering my questions, I had to down the dish that they now pushed in front of me along with a bottle of San Miguel. Eat balut, they said. And drink beer."

Normally, Merina did not eat balut or drink beer. On this particular day, he did both.

"I did so because of my newly adopted-on-the-spot 'eat balut, drink beer' rule. That directive, simply stated, is that when a key source or a table of sources invites me to do something that I do not normally do—and it does not violate my principles—I will indeed eat, drink and be wary. And

I will do so because it makes my sources comfortable. I will imbibe because it demonstrates a willingness to share something that is meaningful to them. And I will partake because, in a small way, it is a signal of acceptance of a part of their culture."

Interruptions

During an interview, interruptions are likely to occur. Book reviewer Charles Claffey once conducted a frenzied interview with Studs Terkel, who is a master interviewer himself as well as a massive juggler of events and conversations.

"During our talk, he fielded about a dozen phone calls, gave taped interviews to a couple of out-of-town radio stations, and initiated several other telephone calls; listened to the tape of his daily radio show; ate lunch; and conducted a brief interview within our interview for a reporter writing about Chicago for a tourists' guide book."

While reporter Gretchen Peters was interviewing Pakistan's interior minister about the capture of top Al Qaeda members for the *Christian Science Monitor*, she was interrupted regularly by the ringing of his cell phone. Except, it wasn't a ring. "It kept playing the theme song from *Mission Impossible*," she said. "I asked him if the music was a commentary on his job. He laughed and said his son had programmed it to play his favorite movie tune."

Check for accuracy as you go

Accuracy is important. Always ask for a business card, which will give you the exact spelling of name, job title, and company name. Ask for copies of annual reports or studies that the subject may talk about during the interview. Sources talking off the tops of their heads may round off figures that do not jibe with the actual report.

Don't pretend to be an expert. Stop your subject when he gives you some complex information. "Let me make sure I understand what you are saying," you can say. Then summarize what he has said and repeat it. This will clear up any misunderstandings that can occur when an interviewer just goes with the flow of a tech-talking source.

Double-check spellings for key words and all names. Is the subject of your story named Smith, Smyth, or Smythe? Norm Moyes, a veteran journalist and educator at Boston University, tells a story about the reporter who did an interview with a subject named Bryan Smith. At the end of their conversation, the reporter inquired, "Do you spell your name with an I or a Y?" "I'm glad you asked,' said the subject. "I use a Y."

Of course, the subject was referring to his first name, the reporter to his last. When the story came out and the spelling was Brian Smyth, the writer got both names wrong.

Finally, remember, the interviewer always rings twice . . . or more. If you have a nagging doubt about some factoid from the interview, call the source back to verify what has been said. The source will appreciate your clearing up possible misunderstandings before they are in print.

How long is an interview?

Interviews can be as short as a single question. "I like it when interviews are brief," said actor Robert DeNiro as he sat down with Cal Fussman for *Esquire* magazine. "Are we done yet?"

Or they can range in duration—from ten to thirty minutes for newspaper work; an hour or two for magazine pieces; and anywhere from five to thirty hours on tape for a major interview, such as one being done for *Playboy*.

Book-length projects can involve much more. Lawrence Grobel sat with John Huston asking him questions for more than a hundred hours over a sixteen-month period for his book-length family portrait, *The Hustons*.

The more time spent interviewing, the more likely it is that you will get more chances to find out how the subject's mind works. Likewise, more than one interview is recommended to increase the range of questions and to form impressions over time. Cover all the bases, especially when there are allegations in the air.

One of longest magazine interviews was *Playboy's* with CNN owner Ted Turner, which began as eight hundred pages of unedited transcript. "Turner's mouth almost never stops," said interviewer Peter Ross Range. Nor does his travel schedule.

"Our interviewing took place on his sailboat, on a motor launch, in various cars, in an airplane, in his office, at his home, in a baseball stadium, in a high school gymnasium and in several restaurants. Since it was impossible to predict what would make the most telling comment, I had to tape everything . . . . At one point, he kept talking to me through an open door while he used the john—as the tape rolled on."

Ending the interview

Try to make the decision to leave a mutual, collaborative one. If you are doing an interview over lunch, "Are we ready to go?" is better than "Let's go." Such prerogatives are best shared, and a subject may resent your usurping any of them.

Knowing when and how to leave makes all the difference in rounding out an interview. In general, a handshake, a thank-you, and a gentle—and genteel—manner will provide an interviewer with easier access the next time around, and always leave the door open for follow-up.

Meantime, keep your mind and your tape recorder working. You never know what might happen as you head toward the door.

One of the most famous exit interviews occurred as Robert Scheer and Barry Golson were exchanging some parting comments in the doorway of presidential candidate Jimmy Carter's home. "We said to Carter, more as a parting comment than anything else, that the topic most of our friends were uneasy about was their perception of the Baptist faith," recalls Golson, "and he went on for another eight or nine minutes to speak about small-town religion, people's frailties and human temptation."

"I've looked on a lot of women with lust," said Jimmy Carter. "I've committed adultery in my heart many times. This is something that God recognizes I will do—and I have done it—and God forgives me for it. But that doesn't mean that I condemn someone who not only looks on a woman with lust but who leaves his wife and shacks up with somebody out of wedlock. Christ says, don't consider yourself better than someone else because one guy screws a whole bunch of women while the other guy is loyal to his wife."

That proved to be a quote heard 'round the world, delivered to alert interviewers who knew how to stretch a long good-bye.

Physical contact: Kissing & beyond

Sometimes kissing is part of the showbiz world of air-kisses and "love ya, baby." People who love being famous also love dispensing hugs—and more—to their fandom. Before her interview with Muhammad Ali, Maureen Dowd was told by the boxer's handlers that he liked to be called Champ, and he liked "to be kissed and flirted with." (The *New York Times* columnist kept the Champ at a distance with a firm write jab.)

Boston Globe columnist Diane White recalls being sent out to interview a 74-year-old Boston pol and occasional mayoral candidate named Dapper O'Neil, who was being treated at a hospital for a pinched nerve in his neck. Dapper was lying on his back, unable to move, his neck in traction. White introduced herself and started to ask him a question.

"First, you'll have to give me a kiss," he said.

"I tried to jolly him out of it," said White, "but he insisted. A kiss or no interview."

Hmmmm. "I suppose that, by today's standards, I was sexually harassed by Dapper, although at the time I thought I was just doing my job," recalled White. Still, the thought of kissing Dapper wasn't a prospect to be relished.

"Then I thought about the deadline looming. I looked down at him lying there in his pajamas, made sure he was immobilized and said to myself, 'Oh, what the hell.' I bent down, kissed him and we got on with the interview."

Later, White realized that she should have left the room as soon as he asked for a kiss. She should have called her editor. "I could have sued the pants, so to speak, off Dapper," she reflected. "I was so young and naive. I remember thinking that I was lucky that all he wanted was a kiss."

Sometimes the reporter–source relationship can blossom into something more intimate—and more troubling—as evidenced by the Suzy Wetlaufer-Jack Welch affair, wherein the *Harvard Business Review* editor ended up as correspondent in the GE head's divorce battle.

Country music writer Nancy Helen Wilson slapped singer Willie Nelson with a $50 million lawsuit in Florida for "breach of promise" in 1990, five years after their affair began in a Biloxi, Mississippi, hotel room where she was supposedly conducting an interview with Nelson.

"From the first moment that he kissed me," she told TV interviewers, "the rest of the world just vanished."

Reporter Soledad O'Brien made a memorable live debut on NBC TV in a sports bar crammed with drunken San Francisco Giants fans in 1993. As she got ready to interview a subject, the man groped her. She froze and forgot her questions.

What did she learn from that episode? "After that, I swore never to do another live shot in a bar," she said, "or, if I had to, to make sure my rear end was against the bar."

The dangers of drink

Freelance writer William J. Slattery, on assignment to profile a celebrated author for *Boston Magazine*, read all of the author's work and all previously published interviews. By the time he showed up to do the interview, Slattery knew the writer's work so intimately that his admiration for both her talent and persona had increased immensely.

Slattery arrived at the author's home on time and fully prepared. She swept grandly into the living room like an actress making an entrance. "Serenity. Composure. Success," said the interviewer. "That's what I think I was meant to see and that's what I saw."

The author took Slattery on a tour of her large and beautiful home and introduced him to various members of her staff. They chatted amiably. "She was pleased that I knew her work. She was gratified that I liked it."

"How about a glass of wine?" the author asked brightly when the tour was over.

"Sure," said Slattery, thinking: interviewing is thirsty work. He turned on a tape recorder and started the conversation.

"People have always talked to me," said Slattery afterward. "I have this great, kind, understanding face, and a compassionate manner." Add to that a bottle of wine, and let the veritas begin.

A few minutes into the first glass, the author relaxed a whole lot. In about a half hour, they had a second glass, and in about forty-five minutes the famous lady author was coming apart. "The sculpted hair was coming down. The careful manner of speech had become informal and then confessional and then, finally, heart-breaking."

Then she launched into a noisy and tearful lament over her marriage, which was failing. "The interview was getting out of hand. She was telling me things about her marriage that I hadn't read or heard anywhere else . . . . Oh, God. Oh, God, she wailed. I think we had some more wine about here."

And so they drank on, like boats bobbing against the current. "She was unburdening herself to me the way a man does to his bartender, completely and without fear of censure or fear that what was being divulged would be repeated," said Slattery. "The woman . . . was now making a spectacle of herself, writing and thrashing about, wringing her hands and weeping."

Suddenly, the author's daughter, alarmed at all the noise, came into the room to see what was the matter. Slattery turned the tape recorder off.

The interview was over.

And so was the story.

Lest he be tempted to use the inebriated material the author had so piteously revealed, Slattery destroyed the tape recording and took a kill fee from the magazine.

CHAPTER 10

The Interviewer as Performer

The world is divided into two basic personality types—actives and passives. Actives usually win. Where does this leave the interviewer? In many situations, the interviewer is in charge, especially if you think of a job interview, a medical interview, a legal interview in a courtroom, or a police interrogation.

But in journalistic situations, is the inquiring reporter in charge? Rarely. More often, you are dependent on the subject's cooperation and limited schedule, not to mention his or her whims and good (or ill) will. In fact, the subject has the right to remain silent, to have a lawyer nearby. Why? Because what he or she says may be used against him in a people's court known as the press and public opinion.

Therefore, the image that you project as an interviewer is key to achieving success when going one-on-one with a subject. Your manner of presentation and delivery can either boost or booby-trap your efforts. Your goal is to establish good rapport and to come across at your best.

But just as we are often surprised by the sound of our own voices on tape recordings, many interviewers would be shocked by the image they are projecting—if videotapes were available afterward.

The interview then is more than a simple process by which we ask questions and get answers. It is a relationship, however brief, between two people in which we use the dynamics of conversation to draw the other person out. It's a conversation, only more so. It calls for intense listening skills, and the interviewer must never forget his or her role—not only as interviewer but, in turn, as performer and audience.

You cannot annoy or pester people into liking you; and you can't fool them into it, either. Being decent, being relentlessly human may get you the interview. But there is a fine line between kindness and weakness in the view of many subjects, and you don't want to be perceived as a pushover.

Should you—as some old journalists suggest—"just be yourself"? The answer is: probably not. It is best to be a performer, to be vigorous. "Every interview is a performance," says Jonathan Schenker, director of media relations for Ketchum PR. "If you are bored, it will be obvious."

Being a performer

Consider yourself as an actor in a long-running Broadway show, or someone who has been touring forever with *Our Town*, playing the same part in the same show a couple hundred times a year. How can you stand it?

Well, the audience changes, the subtleties of the role become more pronounced, and the money is still nicely crazy after all these years. Moreover, while the role doesn't vary much, you are getting increasingly favorable reviews—and you are getting better and better at the task. What you are becoming good at is *performance*.

The conversations over lunch, the chatting with intermediaries, the smiles and handshakes as you sit down to begin the interview—they are all part of the performance, ad-libbed for the occasion but very much the same. Like the stage performer, you have to ask a question without letting on that you have asked it a few hundred times.

It can feel a bit phony at first, but by the hundredth time it feels just like part of what you do. And chances are that if your source has been around for awhile, he has to answer the question without letting on that he's been asked it a few hundred times, too.

So what does that make you? A very effective performer.

If you examine your interviewer image, you can identify four essential components, each of which you must learn to understand, control, and present in a positive manner, much as a performer does.

1. Body language

Is your body saying things that may be sabotaging your message? Some interviewers have unconscious habits, gestures, and mannerisms that detract from their effectiveness. Pencil-fidgeting, ear-pulling, lip-licking, adjusting eyeglasses, stroking a moustache or beard, playing with jewelry, glancing frequently at a wristwatch, or just plain slouching in a chair can be turnoffs for the interviewee.

In general, once you have settled into the interview, you want to be still. Don't fidget, move around, pace, or use elaborate motions. All movements should be intentional, meaningful.

2. Voice

Do you sound good? Listen to yourself objectively. Your credibility as an interviewer depends largely on the manner in which you ask questions. If you have a childish voice, for instance, it can diminish your effectiveness.

If you have a monotone, your questions will seem ponderous and dull. Listen to tapes of your voice, and seek guidance from others who may be aware of any vocal inflections or awkwardness you may have. Then endeavor to achieve a friendly, poised voice that asks questions in a balanced yet bright manner.

As interviewing becomes more of a global preoccupation, the advantage goes to the bilinguist. *ABC News* reporter Paula Zahn used her fluent Spanish to secure exclusive one-on-one interviews with Cuban leader Fidel Castro during a trip to Havana by a huge U.S. television-news squad. Zahn's achievement stood out during a week when other U.S. network stars were interviewing anyone in Cuba who could speak English—including one another.

3. Appearance

Clothing, hairstyle, and makeup can either emphasize what is flattering in you, or they can be a distraction. Strive for a professional look on the job. When choosing clothing, think ahead and dress appropriately.

Veteran farm editors bring work clothes when they show up to interview farmers during planting season. They know that they will have to accompany a farmer into the fields at three or four o'clock in the morning, which is when the day begins in a race against the noonday sun.

In general, it helps to be ready to participate, if needed, in daily activities. To interview ex-Detroit Tigers catcher Lance Parrish when Parrish was undergoing back rehabilitation, a columnist jumped into the pool where Parrish was swimming laps. They spoke between strokes.

Lawrence Grobel once reflected that in order to get stories he has had to learn to skydive, has been strapped into a trotter's sulky, and has taken courses in karate and transcendental meditation. "But no matter what else I've done, the most crucial part . . . has been to get people to talk."

4. Confidence

When you are maximizing your positive traits, and when you believe in what you are doing, you exude confidence. The aroma is intoxicating.

When you are self-assured, your subjects have confidence in you and in the outcome. For your part, you speak and move in a more comfortable manner. You are less tense. The quality of rapport goes up dramatically, and the interview is going to be better as a result.

Self-confidence is achieved through a variety of methods, but for the interviewer there is one key ingredient: preparation. If you have done your homework, and if you are ready for an interview, you will be confident as you knock on the door.

The way you walk into a room or an office creates a halo effect. Don't slouch. Be positive, confident, enthusiastic. Believe in what you are doing, and your subject will pick up on that feeling immediately.

It's contagious.

CHAPTER 11

The Art of Listening

A good interviewer is someone who listens for a living. The *Wall Street Journal* once profiled 78-year-old Marian Houghton, a feature writer for the *Jaffrey-Rindge Chronicle*, a 1,500-circulation weekly in Jaffrey, New Hampshire. "I try to limit myself to ten stories a week plus the columns," she told Ellen Graham of the *Journal*. "Everybody has a story in their own funny way. There's something in there that they didn't know they had until you let them talk."

How does Mrs. Houghton do it?

"I listen," she says. "I keep my eyes open and my ears flappin'."

TV and radio correspondent Charles Osgood told interviewer Marian Christy that he got his best ideas by listening to what people say. "To be a good listener, you have to shut up and listen," he says.

"That's how you get insight, by listening. When I listen to my kids, I try to hear what they're trying to say. When I listen to my wife, I hear what's between the lines. Reaction is vital to being a good listener. You have to act as if what's being discussed is the most important thing in the world."

For the interviewer, aggressive listening is the difference between success and failure on the job. There have been numerous instances of tin-eared listeners and famous misquotes.

"I gave a speech in which I said that every morning of my life I wake up feeling as though I weighed 300 pounds and was $8^{1}/_{2}$ months pregnant," said Colleen McCullough, author of *The Thorn Birds*. "I was talking about creative energies and all that.

"Naturally, the press picked it up, and *People* magazine reported, 'Millionaire author Colleen McCullough boasts that she is 8½ months pregnant.' They wouldn't apologize, either. I'm not pregnant. I'm not a single parent. Such are the hazards of fame and fortune."

When basketball star Larry Bird was a senior at Indiana State University, he was asked by a reporter how he made up for lost time in the classroom when traveling with the basketball team. Specifically, the reporter wanted to know about taking exams. "Oh, the coach takes care of that," said Bird.

He meant that coach Bill Hodges made arrangements for makeup work. When the story came out, however, the reporter quoted Bird as though the coach were doing something devious, giving an athlete preferential treatment with under-the-table tactics. For the rest of the season, Larry Bird refused to give print interviews. He would only do television interviews, where, for better or worse, his answers would be his own, and not subject to the risk of misinterpretation by a reporter who wasn't listening carefully or following up with questions for clarifying details.

Listening requires intense concentration. A good definition of concentration for journalists is that articulated by "business philosopher" Jim Rohn: "Wherever you are, be there!" Listening well engenders a sense of intimacy. "There is something seductive about the interview process," says Terry Gross, host of *Fresh Air*, the public radio interview show known for its engaging conversations with authors and newsmakers. "People might be thinking how nice it would be to have someone who listened that completely."

"You must listen with your blood," acting coach Stella Adler said, describing the level of intensity required to play a part.

Looking closely at the different numbers involved in speech and listening abilities, however, points to the crux of the problem. We can comprehend up to 600 words per minute. But the average speaker talks at a rate of only 200 words per minute. A slow speaker may speak at 150 words per minute.

Thus, we have anywhere from three to four times the amount of time we need to understand what is being said during an interview. That leaves plenty of time for tuning out. In one test, Ivy League college students checked out with only a 25 percent listening rate in the classroom; that is, they failed to retain 75 percent of what was said during a talk.

Some interviewers will turn on a tape recorder and tune out of their own interviews. They maintain occasional eye contact, nod their head from time to time, and even ask questions—but they don't listen aggressively. For them, listening is a passive act. They assume that the tape recorder is capturing everything; they can listen more attentively to the tapes later at the office.

This approach is self-destructive. Don't leave your own interview by daydreaming, fantasizing, or relying on the tape recorder to do your job for you. If you aren't vigilant, and especially if you are interviewing someone who is a bit of a bore, your brain begins to wander. And that quote—perhaps that one key quotable phrase that will make all the difference—passes there in front of your ears, and you miss it because your mind is somewhere else. Your worst enemy on an interview is often your own brain. So you have to work at overcoming that natural tendency.

An interviewer is someone who gets paid for listening. Unfortunately, someone with an active imagination may find their thoughts jumping from one thing to the next, going off easily on tangents. The more imaginative you are, and the less experience you have as an interviewer, the more likely you are to drift from the scene of your own interview.

What interviewers need are less imagination and more ability to focus hard on the job at hand. To be a good listener means more than just asking questions; it means being attentive, leaning forward, nodding, and making sounds or gestures of approval. A good listener is active, not passive.

Street smarts for interviewers

"I think very often people don't listen enough," Mark McCormack, author of *What They Don't Teach You at Harvard Business School*, told an interviewer. "I think they have a preconceived idea of what they're going to do and what the other person is going to do and don't pay any attention to the signs that are there which might indicate that something is amiss or something is going in another direction."

In his book, McCormack preaches the importance of using street smarts as opposed to classroom techniques. "Much of what I say and do in business, from a self-effacing comment to an intentionally provocative one, is designed to give myself a slight psychological edge over others, or to help me get the most out of others," he says. "That is what street smarts really are: an applied people sense."

How can this help interviewers?

"Listen aggressively," says McCormack. "Listen not only to what some-one is saying but to how he is saying it. People tend to tell you a lot more than they mean to. Keep pausing—a slightly uncomfortable silence will make them say even more."

When Clay Felker was editor of *Esquire*, for instance, Aaron Latham, then working for the *Washington Post*, interviewed him. Felker, a veteran of the publishing wars, was completely disarmed by Latham's listening tech-nique. Latham would ask a question, then wait for an answer. Even if the interviewee didn't want to respond, Latham would sit there patiently and silently wait until the subject eventually started to talk.

"I was so impressed," said Felker, " I offered him a job on the spot, and we have been working together off and on ever since."

So why do some interviewers turn a deaf ear on the subject while oth-ers are getting an earful of great quotes? They listen aggressively. "People are constantly revealing themselves in ways that will go unnoticed," said Mark McCormack, "unless you are aggressively involved in noticing them."

Tips on listening aggressively

- First, understand the problem of your own tendency to drift or lose focus, as your brain skips ahead or off on tangents. Don't give in to imag-ination. Stay in the moment. Remind yourself to stay alert.

- If a subject is dull, don't tune out. Instead, ask yourself this question: "What's in this for my reader?" Turn the topic in that direction.

- If the subject is a slow speaker, don't use the time to daydream. Instead, capitalize on the fact that thought is faster than speech. Listen between lines to the tone of the speaker's voice, and use the time to challenge, to anticipate, to mentally summarize and weigh the evidence you are sorting as you move from topic to topic.

- If a subject's delivery is poor, don't let the sloppy syntax turn you off. Instead, judge the content for its own sake. Take notes in your own style, quoting minimally for effect.

- If a subject is biased, hold your fire. Don't enter into an argument. Don't react to emotional words. Keep your mind open and withhold judgment until your comprehension is complete. Then debate politely for clarification, if the topic requires a full airing. Remember that your goal during an interview is to gather information, not to win debaters' points. (As F. Scott Fitzgerald once noted: "Remember this—if you shut your mouth, you have your choice.")

- Listen for ideas and central themes, not for isolated facts. Don't focus on minutiae. You may be missing the big story altogether.

- Take notes, but don't get hung up on the note-taking process. Don't let note-taking interfere with maintaining eye contact with the subject, either. "The most fertile, consistent, revealing arena for observation is the eyes," says Mark McCormack. "Remember that people communicate with their eyes when they can't use words."

- Don't fake attention; work at it. Exhibit an active body state, not a listening slouch. Show energy. Show excitement about the topic and the person being interviewed. This will be transferred to the interviewee, and his or her speech will become livelier.

- Don't give in to distractions, even if they are coming from the subject. Concentrate on what is being said, regardless of the interviewee's mannerisms and quirky habits.

- And don't forget that sometimes you—yes, you—are to blame for a subject's seeming tediousness. Are your questions interesting enough? Do they encourage the subject to give insightful answers or merely rhetorical statements, company slogans, or dull statistics? The way you phrase a question can make the difference between a lively response and a dull one.

- If you sit too long in the same spot, it gets harder to pay attention. If your attention begins to flag, make up an excuse to take a quick break. Request a minute-long break to get a drink of water, wash your hands, make a quick phone call—anything to get up and move around and get the blood moving. Then, sit down again, if possible on a different chair to try to see things from a different angle.

Finally, know when it pays not to listen. When a fireworks factory blew up, Marian Houghton, our intrepid feature writer for the *Jaffrey-Rindge Chronicle*, got the story by getting to the scene for interviews ahead of the fire trucks. "I made believe I was deaf to get by the cops," she confessed afterward.

CHAPTER 12

Conquering Shyness

For journalists who are expected to conduct interviews, shyness can be a major obstacle on the job. Collectively, an estimated 40 percent of the population is shy, to one degree or another. For 10 percent to 20 percent, it's an inherited personality trait. The others have what researchers in social psychology at Stanford University call "late-developing shyness," which results in them being fearful or timid when meeting strangers.

Shyness causes the heart rate and blood pressure to rise, and pupils will dilate at a faster rate than for those less inhibited. This can stand in the way of shy people making eye contact, expressing opinions, and communicating effectively with others, especially authorities. Those suffering from shyness tend not to smile. They are reluctant to take risks. Being so concerned about being accepted and liked, they may go along with many things that they might not approve of at a personal level.

Shy people also have difficulty handling intimate situations, and intimacy is often what great interviews are all about. Being shy, however, does not necessarily mean that you lack confidence or the ability to conduct successful interviews. Many successful communicators who describe themselves as shy have learned to cope with it, including Johnny Carson, Barbara Walters, Gloria Steinem, and Garrison Keillor.

While some shy people deal with their anxieties by withdrawing from human contact, journalists have to learn how to combat and overcome shyness. It can be done.

One key symptom of shyness that can affect interviewing performance is the tendency for shy people to worry excessively about how they appear to others. Consequently they may become self-absorbed, causing them to miss what others are saying. Furthermore, they may be perceived as being aloof, or not very good at listening, the key role of the interviewer.

"When you're anxious, you just want to get your agenda over with and get the hell out of there," one shy subject told *Wall Street Journal* columnist Hal Lancaster, who has coped with shyness on the job himself.

"While formal interviews don't bother me," he said, "working a room of strangers—mandatory stuff for a reporter—has never come naturally."

Practice helps

Psychologists have found that shy youngsters whose parents gently push them to try new things and to overcome their fears are less likely to be inhibited than are children whose parents overprotect them. Similarly, for the shy interviewer, the best way to overcome interview phobia is to just do interviews, however difficult they may be at the outset.

In other words, to overcome shyness, you want to look for opportunities to practice the craft of asking questions, gradually working up to doing interviews until they seem to come naturally. The key is "to take that terrifying first step, the shy person's bête noire," adds columnist Hal Lancaster. "And usually, the only way to do it is just to do it."

Wellesley College psychologist Jonathan Cheek, in his book *Conquering Shyness: The Battle Anyone Can Win* (written with his sister and research coordinator, Rowena Cheek) has compiled practical tips to help shy adults overcome their sometimes-crippling anxieties. An optimistic outlook is key.

Instead of saying, "I'm not comfortable doing interviews, so I'm sure I'll bungle it," tell yourself: "With each interview, I become more relaxed and become better at doing my job."

If you are persistent, success can be built on small failures and frustration, even catastrophe. When you make a mistake—recognize it, learn from it, and move on. Shyness doesn't have to be a permanent condition. Learn to accept feedback, even from yourself, on practice interviews. By looking for points of gradual improvement, you can learn how to approach people with more confidence. Over time and with practice, a reporter can develop the verbal skills, body language, and sense of social timing that can ease the way for effective interviews.

"Many people can be helped by making a commitment to changing their shyness—putting in the same effort required to overcome other problem behaviors such as overeating or smoking," psychologist Philip Zimbardo told *U.S. News & World Report*.

The authors of *Conquering Shyness* recommend practicing by picking nonthreatening social situations, like a coffee break with colleagues, to observe the people in the group around you. Without staring, take note of their postures, mannerisms, and facial expressions. Listen carefully to what they are saying, and write down your observations in detail later.

Not only will this exercise help you realize that the people you may have once feared are not saying anything particularly brilliant or unique, but it should also help you become a more active listener and conversationalist. That is what interviewing is all about.

Ultimately, by looking for chances to practice doing interviews in nonthreatening situations, accepting small failures as part of the learning curve, and building up your skills to observe, record, and participate in conversations, you will be able to approach interview settings will less anxiety. With practice, comfort and confidence will gradually increase.

Relaxation methods

Researchers also recommend learning some relaxation method, such as meditation or self-hypnosis. Then, practice that relaxation technique while visualizing all the steps leading up to your next interview. It's not unlike someone who is afraid of giving a speech. Eventually, you can teach yourself to relax automatically when called upon to perform your job.

Bear in mind that even veteran interviewers are often anxious when meeting someone important or intimidating for the first time. The adrenaline flows, resulting in familiar symptoms: palpitations, a tremulous voice, constricted breathing, and butterflies in the stomach.

For dealing with jitters, learn to breathe deeply, with long inhales and exhales. When you inhale, visualize how you are taking in everything your body craves: oxygen, purity, strength, resolve, new beginnings.

When you exhale, you are removing toxins, negativity, carbon dioxide, and stress—everything your body wants to shed. Exhale twice as long as you inhale. A brief breathing exercise is surprisingly effective at neutralizing the jitters whenever they arise.

Other recommendations include taking acting classes. The regimen will likely include breathing exercises, dealing with stage fright, and in essence learning how to pretend to be someone else. Actors rely on scripts; this is also a good approach to interviewing for the shy journalist. Prepare specific question to ask and write them out on index cards before the interview.

"You may look robotic," says Hal Lancaster, "but that's better than tongue-tied."

Being well prepared for your interview helps develop your belief that you will do well, just as studying for an exam gives you confidence that you will perform better when you walk into an examination room to take a test.

Projecting a sense of confidence

Don't let shyness hold back your sense of confidence. Foremost, you must believe in what you are doing and that you have the skills to do a good job even if you are shy. In fact, because they speak less, shy interviewers are often very good listeners. The key to a successful interview is often the ability to listen attentively and confidently and to show interest when someone else talks.

Overall, an aura of confidence makes you more appealing to others, who judge the "inner you" by your external demeanor.

Before you even enter the room, imagine the situation that you are anticipating. Rehearse the interview mentally. Imagine the give and take of the exchange, with the desired positive outcome.

Throw away any fearful hesitations by remembering that the person being interviewed probably has no particular expectation of the outcome of this interview and is willing to help the interview go well. Indeed, there is a greater burden on the interview subject to answer intelligently, while you have your list of good, solid questions well prepared.

When you project confidence mentally, you will reduce the anxiety level for all concerned. Entering the room in a confident manner starts things off on the right foot.

How to interview shy subjects

The shy subject is often someone who has made a sharp dichotomy between the public, "working" self that he or she lets others see—as a business-person, celebrity, or whatever—and the private self, which that person may keep hidden. In fact, it is often difficult to break through to the private person because the public self serves as a shield.

Shy subjects must be approached differently. Though they do not want to draw attention to themselves, they often want to be noticed, even to be considered outstanding. But they do not want to take risks. Thus is born an internal conflict.

They often set unattainable standards of perfection for themselves. But they also tend to be egotistical, so they often fall short of that perfect ideal. They are not particularly sociable and may choose to keep a low personal profile.

"A great many theatrical performers I have interviewed are shy, but virtually all shy people I know are performers in this sense," says psychologist Philip Zimbardo. He points out that:

> That's the result, in many cases, of adults making it clear to a child that self-worth depends on current performance: "Mamma won't love you if you don't do this." "Daddy won't like you if you don't make the Little League." "The teacher won't respect you if you can't memorize the poem." You are accepted—or, worse, rejected—according to whether you meet your most recent sales quota, whether you get into college, whether you're the prettiest girl on the block, whether you make the team, etcetera.

To interview a shy subject, the line of questioning should work at integrating the two selves, mindful that shy subjects tend to be more dissatisfied and have lower morale in their work settings. They require praise.

Questions posed to them should make it clear that their contributions are being recognized, that life is not passing them over with its rewards. Also, look for ways to communicate that their worth as a person is independent of their latest sales achievement or sporting feat or good looks.

CHAPTER 13

Note-Taking & Recording Techniques

Tom Hunter called it casual interviewing. "All day long, quotes are swirling around you in bits of conversation, or you're observing interesting scenes and happenings," he said. "Develop an ear and an eye for them, make note of them, and you quickly build a storehouse of quotes and anecdotes you can draw on to feed into articles you might not be writing for months or even years."

A photographer came into Hunter's office one day to present his portfolio. As he laid out his photos, he said, "I understand you're a photographer, too."

"Oh, I'm just an amateur," said Hunter.

"Don't ever apologize for being an amateur," said the photographer, who stopped what he was doing and pointedly added: "The word comes from the French, you know, and it means lover. So, you love photography, and if you ever got involved with it professionally you might find you didn't even like it anymore."

When he left, Hunter wrote it down. He used that quote, or part of it, in three different stories he wrote over the years. "Perhaps you're working on a story and haven't been able to get a good quotable quote, or you don't have time to interview for one," said Hunter. When that happens, "It might be in your [note] cards."

Keep a notebook handy

An employee at the Patuxent River Naval Air Station in Maryland was in a local hardware store one Saturday morning when a squadron of F-14 fighter jets flew over. They made a horrendous noise and startled another customer, who asked, "What was that?" The naval employee answered, "Sounds like freedom to me."

Then someone tapped him on the shoulder. He turned, and there was novelist Tom Clancy, who said, "I'm going to use that line in a book I'm writing. Give me your name and address, and I'll send you an autographed copy." He did.

For the interviewer, the lesson is clear: never go anywhere without a pad and pencil. If you are out with friends for an evening, someone will say something memorable. Write it down. If you need it, it's there.

Of course, taking notes is rarely jotting down one-liners overheard at a hardware store. More often, it means listening to a source who may be talking fast . . . or s-l-o-w . . . and who may be saying something quite interesting . . . or d-u-l-l . . . while you attempt to keep pace and jot down the highlights.

Things can go wrong even in this simple process, of course. At the *Cincinnati Enquirer*, the story is told of the late and usually astounding theater critic E. B. "Rad" Radcliffe, who had arranged for two telephone interviews from Hollywood to come to his home one evening. When the first call came in, Rad found only two sheets of paper next to the phone. He covered both sides of both pages with notes written in blue ballpoint ink. The second call came in just as the first interview was completed, and Radcliffe could not find more paper. He did, however, find another pen— with red ink.

Next day he displayed his interview notes for the dueling dialogues. Both sides of both pages were completely filled with alternating lines of red and blue notes and quotes.

Taking notes is a tedious part of the interviewing process. But you not only have to be a good reporter and writer; you may also have to be a good witness in court some future day defending what you wrote. It pays to train and tighten memory, of course, for that day when note-taking is not possible. One good practice is to try writing a draft of your story without referring to your notes. Then go back and check your notes for accuracy.

Such training improves the memory for dialogue and facts. Your waiter at a restaurant, for instance, may seem to have an incredible memory; from long practice, experienced waitstaff can confidently remember orders without jotting a note. Others in the service world—bartenders, bellhops, and the like—can often recall names and faces from years back. Why can't interviewers be that way?

Some are. Will McDonough, the fabled sports reporter for the *Boston Globe*, was never seen taking notes while talking to a source. His school of reporting—"no notes are good notes," if you will—would be considered dangerous today. However, many of McDonough's sources were high-end professional team owners and athletes, who thought they were talking to God—a god, in his case, who usually called back to check the quotes, and liked to work off the record.

The problem for most writers, however, is overload: a combination of too much to recall and too many lawyers to answer to if the quotes don't match the notes and someone complains. That is why it is important to take careful and complete notes; they are the quick safety net below the wire if a source hollers, "I was misquoted!"

To quote verbatim or paraphrase

"Am I going too fast?" asked author Neil Sheehan, as a reporter took notes the old-fashioned way. Such subjects are considerate, but that is not always the case. Note-taking can be problematical with subjects who have a heavy accent, who talk fast, who like to name-drop and chatter.

Moreover, can one listen and write at the same time? No. First you must listen, then you must write, unless your eye/ear/hand control is exceptional.

Note-taking on the keyboard of a laptop can expedite matters. This is often possible on phone interviews, for instance, especially if you invest is an inexpensive headset that allows your hands to be free from holding the telephone. Shorthand is another solution. Tom Wolfe, for instance, uses the Gregg system (which may help explain the hallmark extensive quotes he often brings into his writing).

One trick of the trade: if you can't keep up with a speed-talking subject, toss out an easy question—and while he is holding forth on that, take notes on the previous question.

Remember that there is no need to take notes verbatim. You are a reporter, not a courtroom stenographer. Many interviewers take keyword notes, then fill in and expand on them immediately after the interview from memory. During your interview, of course, always mark any direct quotes with quotation marks. Then, you can get back to your source later to double-check the exact wording on quotes you know will be used in the story. Get the quote right.

Some interviews give you great quotes. Others give you great impressions; these are best captured through description and paraphrase. "I never did believe in that so-called accurate note-taking and quoting verbatim," says Gay Talese, a strong advocate of getting a good earful and then using a paraphrase.

"It wasn't always that accurate," he says, recalling how reporters for different newspapers would cover the same press conference and come away with different quotes.

For Talese, the problem is understandable. People often talk funny, and it can look odd when seen in print. Often, writers help them out by cleaning up quotes, making them more grammatical, so that the sources look reasonably intelligent and readers can comprehend what is being said.

"If you quote me directly," says Talese, "some paragraphs will get a sense of what I am saying, but in others you will find that the sentence structure is somewhat reversed. You can understand me, but when you try to put this on the written page, I will not communicate well. That's why, if you were to do what I did—write a series of interviews for a magazine story or a book—you would be wise to take the essence of what I am saying and put it in your own words. It will read better."

Then there is, too, the matter of style. "Why do we have to stick to other people's words? Particularly when we're the writers. Let's put the story in our own words—that's how we can communicate more fully and more accurately. At least, I can. That's why I got away from using direct quotes," says Talese, "although I always attribute material to the proper source."

Bruce Weber of the *New York Times* captured the mannerisms of Celine Dion as she got ready to open a new kind of show in Las Vegas. Weber found that he could not spend time around Dion without being struck "by the lavish coronation of a slightly built, French Canadian pop diva who is about to turn 35 and, in person, is disconcertingly chatty and displays the meandering focus and restless body language of a teenager."

"If there is such a thing as being authentically artificial," wrote Weber, "that's what she is, and it is rather sweet." Then he turns his paraphrase camera on his subject:

> She looks around as she talks, grimaces, scratches her head, runs her hands through her blond and newly tomboyish coif. You don't have to ask her questions; she talks. About her two-year-old son, who has made everything else in life secondary; about her fans and how they can see she is a real person and not just a distant star; about how fortunate she is to have this opportunity at Caesars to do the kind of show she couldn't do on the road and can have a home life as well; about how difficult it is to perform while war is going on.

Advantages of tape recording

The major problem with note-taking is that it impedes our ability to perform Job #1: listen. Note-taking requires you to juggle things, looking at your notes and trying to write while listening to a source race ahead with the answer to your last question, as you try to contemplate the next. Focusing on any one need can diminish the others. Thankfully, the tape recorder is a modern third ear. With a tape recorder, more questions can be asked, and the text of answers is likely to be longer, fuller.

It's easier to use the tape recorder to capture an interview under special conditions, such as a meal at a restaurant, when your hands are busy and taking notes would be cumbersome. Also, editors feel safer if a writer uses a recorder, especially if a publication has been in a lawsuit or had to deal with a source who claimed he was misquoted.

Some subjects are perplexed if you don't have one on the job. Gary Cartwright arranged an interview with actor Gary Busey for a story in

Texas Monthly. The actor had played Lubbock's own Buddy Holly (thus the Texas connection)—and had recently nearly died from an overdose of cocaine and whiskey. This was his first interview since that episode and his subsequent arrest.

By prearrangement, the questions were limited. "The only reason he is talking to me," wrote Cartwright, "is that I promised to ask no questions about his long and much-publicized addiction to drugs and alcohol but to focus instead on his 1978 role in maybe the best rock-and-roll movie ever made, *The Buddy Holly Story*." Unfortunately, Cartwright failed to bring a tape recorder on the set, and Busey, a veteran of the talk-show promotional circuit, complained because he was used to speaking in "bites."

"I have to keep slowing down so you can take notes," he groused. "I lose my train of thought."

Cartright noticed that while Busey sipped only root beer during the interview, he frequently excused himself to use the bathroom. Then it was "bite on":

"It was an honor to be chosen to represent Buddy Holly's artistic purpose," said Busey, leaning toward Cartwright as though he were a camera and this was a close-up, "to wrap myself around the essence of the material and play it full and honest, which is the essence of my performing ability—I'm not conscious of anything between the word 'action' and the word 'cut,' the Panavision camera picks up one thing and one thing only and that's truth—and to make a historical statement about Buddy Holly's connection to rock 'n' roll and do it honestly."

Busey paused. "Did you get that?" he asked. "That's a bite."

Limitations of tape recording

Never depend on a recorder absolutely. Even if the recorder doesn't break down, you will need notes on the subject's attitude, attire, and the overall atmosphere.

There is also the chance that a subject (unless it's Gary Busey), knowing fully well that you are going to use a recorder, will change his mind and ask you to turn it off. Then the note-taking begins.

If a subject wants to go "off the record" while you are taping, turn the tape recorder off. It is advisable to tell the subject at the outset, "If you want to go off the record, just hit the 'off' switch here, so that everything I have on tape is on the record." That makes it nice and easy for future editing when you are in playback and developing your story notes.

Some publications require tapes—such as the *National Enquirer*, after losing a lawsuit or two. Yes, inquiring editors want to know exactly what was said during the interview. They don't want to be in the position of having to trust reporters' notes or memories, especially in the event of a court challenge.

Transcribing

Afterward, listen and transcribe while the material is fresh. You will hear more on a tape transcribed within twenty-four hours than you will hear five or six days later. Accuracy goes to the swiftest. The tape won't necessarily fade, but your memory—and your ability to recall the nuances—will.

Ron Rosenbaum, an investigative journalist whose specialty is explicating what is often beneath the surface, finds it difficult to focus on the subtleties of an idea being discussed during an interview—because, after all, he's got an interview to do.

"I'm always too on edge in the course of doing an interview, too busy worrying about my next question, too worried about whether the tape is running, to really hear the interview, to really listen to what's going on, to take note of what the verbal tics, recurrent phrases, rhetorical devices, and slips of the tongue sometimes reveal," he says.

Thus, he says the real value of a recorded interview occurs later when you can study the give and take, putting it in full perspective. "I'm always amazed to discover, on reading the transcript of an interview over for a third time, how much more emerges in some slip or tic, the shadow of some submerged truth that belies the surface intention of the words."

A warning: spell-check programs won't catch gaffes like the following from the Corrections Department at the *New Yorker*:

> In "The Devil's Accountant," a quote from Nathan Glazer about Zellig Harris, Noam Chomsky's teacher, should have read "we all felt his range was enormous," not "we all felt his rage was enormous."

Handling a tape recorder

Maybe it's one of those left-brain/right-brain things, but many fine writers and interviewers are just a bit klutzy when handling a tape recorder. There may even be a direct and inverse relationship between reporting or writing skills and mechanical know-how: the greater the writer, the less likely it is that person can reset the time on a VCR, let alone handle the intricacies of a tape recorder.

Tips & Guidelines

Here are some tips and guidelines that should ease the way as you make your own forays into the reporting wars, tape recorder in hand.

1. Get permission to record.

Never assume the subject is going to agree to being recorded. Ask in advance. Why? First, a tape recording gives an editor peace of mind about the accuracy of quotes used in the story, making it unlikely that a source will be able to holler, "I was misquoted!" If your editor insists on the interview being recorded, you want to know in advance if the subject will be agreeable to its use.

Second, it is unethical (and illegal in many states) to make secret recordings—easily done on the phone, for instance. So always tell a subject in advance that you will be using a recorder.

2. Prepare to deal with "mike fright."

If a subject balks at the idea of your recording an interview, point out that you are doing so in order to be 100 percent accurate. Also point out that taping the interview will save time for the subject as you won't be slowing her or him down to take notes.

Finally, reassure the subject that you are using the tape recorder as a notebook, and no one is going to hear the recording except yourself. Offer to make a copy of the tape for the subject's file, if that would make things more comfortable for all.

3. Create a ready-to-go kit.

Use good equipment, and equip your kit with plenty of backup gear, including an extra tape recorder. Don't skimp. You don't want to risk losing an interview due to a jammed tape, batteries that die, or a recorder that goes clunk and stops in its tracks because of cheap workmanship.

Keep your interviewing equipment in your office in a "toolkit" for speed and safekeeping. A gym or airline travel bag, or an old briefcase, can be used to store recorder, tapes, extra batteries, extension cords, notebooks, pens (in case the subject doesn't want to be recorded and asks you to turn off the tape recorder). It should be ready to go on a moment's notice.

If the equipment is company-owned and must be shared with other writers, put a check-in/check-out sheet on a nearby bulletin board so that interviewers know who has the kit at all times.

4. Test the machine before you start the interview.

At the beginning of the interview, always test your equipment. Include the source in this process so that you have a vocal sound check. "This is Joe Bulldog, talking with Mr. Hot Source on May 15 in Boston," you might say into the microphone. Then ask Mr. Source to say something, and then play it back for review before pushing on with the interview.

You can also use this introductory banter to get the source's permission to record the interview on tape, a good thing to have if there are legal repercussions afterward.

5. Choose the right extras.

Recorders come in all sizes and price ranges. Choose one that is affordable and manageable for you, but try to include three extras that are interviewer friendly:

- A gauge that indicates battery strength.

- Automatic reverse, so that the tape doesn't have to be turned manually when it reaches the end of side one.

- An external microphone that can override the condenser mike built into most recorders today. Condenser microphones work nicely in 75 percent of interviews. But when there is background noise, you need to plug in a "hand-held" mike (actually they are tiny, something you can snake across the table in a crowded restaurant, for instance) to get the source's voice without the intrusion of crowd or workplace noise.

For an interview with Atlanta Braves owner Ted Turner, Peter Ross Range visited the owner's posh office overlooking the playing field at Atlanta Stadium. Turner pressed his nose to the picture window facing the ball field, talking for all he was worth, but Range couldn't hear a word. Later, the tape at that point revealed only an unidentified voice picked up by the condenser mike, saying, "Look at that fool; he never stops."

6. Go beyond the quotes.

While a tape recorder will capture a source's words, you need to capture his spirit. This means color, detail, and character. The more complete and precise the notes, the better the story. No matter how you do it—the important thing is to get notes that go beyond quotes.

One method is to use the recorder as a running notebook. Talk details into it.

Otherwise, use your notebook to jot down circumstances of the room setting, the interviewee, the weather outside, anything that might spice up your story. Often these details can be sprinkled through your story as lead-ins to set up quotes, making the reader feel like he or she has been there and is seeing what you see, as well as hearing what you hear.

7. Keep a handwritten index as you record.

Start each side of each cassette at zero on your tabulator, and keep a handwritten running index to the content as the interview moves along. This will take a lot of the chore work out of finding items in your interview later. It allows you to revisit good quotes or complicated stories quickly; this is important if you have to turn the story in soon. Also, your outline becomes part of your working notes for the story.

This is also a good place to include notes on gestures, mannerisms, and details that enable you to create a scene for readers, not just a litany of quotes.

8. Copy your copy.

It is recommended professional practice to make a duplicate copy of each tape before you start replaying it to transcribe or write out notes. Rewinding and replaying a tape can create wear, and even breakage.

When buying cassette tapes, look for those manufactured with screws, not glued together. They are easier to open up if they become jammed.

If a tape has sensitive information, it is even more important to make a duplicate copy for safekeeping.

9. Don't spindle or reuse.

How long should you keep tapes? Taped interviews should be kept on file for as long as necessary to support a story. Magazine editors often ask that they be submitted with a story for fact-checking and accuracy. Someone may claim that he or she has been misquoted years after a story has run; if this occurs, the editor will want to revisit the taped archives.

In short, don't toss or record over the evidence. At the outset of an assignment, ask the editor if there is a statute of limitations for purposes of legal recall. The tapes may be your property, but they must remain available to the publication if necessary.

10. Leave the door open.

At the end of the interview, be sure to get complete information on your source—e-mail address, cell phone, home phone (to be used in emergency only), travel plans, and anything else that will allow you to get in touch on short notice.

Ask the subject if it's okay to get back to him or her for follow-up, just in case something crucial is missing or needs to be double-checked. (That may cover something as basic as discovering that you have a faulty tape that is not in listenable condition.) Thus, if you have an afterthought or—horrors—the dog has eaten your recorder, or if something has gone wrong mechanically, you can e-mail, call, or return for a follow-up session and stay on deadline with your story.

All in all, the advantages of tape-recording interviews seem self-evident. Subjects tend to give more careful, honest replies when they know they are being taped. And legally, you are more protected (or at least insulated) from lawsuits brought by subjects who claim they have been misquoted or quoted out of context—an old lament, but one too readily believed by a public today that has a scornful opinion of the media.

One final benefit: as you replay your tapes to prepare transcripts of key passages, you will get an unparalleled opportunity to hear yourself in action. This is a great way to refine your own interviewing techniques.

Remember that there is no such thing as a bad interview. In each and every case, an interview offers an opportunity to listen and learn from what worked and what didn't.

CHAPTER 14

Getting the Good Quote

What makes a good quote? A subject who is lively and quotable, first, and an interviewer who knows what to do when a good quote comes along. I.e., pounce on it! Editors love good quotes because they bring personality to a story, and because a good quote is often remembered long after the story has been forgotten.

Old quotes are often good quotes. If you are interviewing a subject who has a history of giving interviews or performing admirably (or notoriously) in the past, you can put those old quotes to use as a lively sidebar. In fact, the quotes don't even have to be from the mouth of the subject. *People* magazine did a story on Liz Taylor and ran a reprise called "How Tongues Wagged About Liz: 43 Years of Abuse." Here are a few of the unattributed quotes:

> Liz has more chins than the Hong Kong phone book.

> Her thighs are so big they're going condo.

> She looks like two small boys fighting under a mink blanket.

> Liz has had so much rice thrown at her she's been named to the board of Uncle Ben's.

> She's all calories, cleavage, and camp.

A good quote is usually short—twenty words or less. It is candid, revealing, and delivered with punch. Sometimes a "bleep" is necessary if the quote is *too* candid or punchy.

You can't predict when you will get good quotes during interviews. In general, they are delightful happenings for the inquiring reporter. You keep priming the pump with lively questions, and you hope some lively stuff comes back, not knowing whether a response is going to hit you in the funnybone or right between the eyes.

You will be pleased to learn that businessmen, tired of being labeled dull by interviewers, are endeavoring to be livelier during interviews. In *The Executive's Guide to Handling a Press Interview*, a popular manual for company heads, author Dick Martin urges executives to remember that news is supposed to be newsy.

Martin quotes a communications expert who says, "Business people should see themselves as experts who can answer who, what, where, when and how. The secret of performing well here is to be quotable, to be able to express facts succinctly in terms that are meaningful to wide audiences and in words that produce maximum impact."

How do words produce maximum impact? Let us count the ways. Good quotes are often statements followed by interjections—real wowers! Or they can be disagreements with prevailing sentiments on any given topic. They can be bits of trade wisdom, the unwritten rules of the business game. They can be cool statistics that knock you off your chair.

They can be predictions, little enumerations and checklists, or private fears. Or impossible demands, pleas, requests, expectations . . . or embarrassing moans when someone's hand is caught in the wrong cookie jar.

There are probably a hundred different categories for the gathering and dispensing of good quotes. Here is a brief refresher course on what to listen for.

The inside angle

A good quote offers contrast to the public persona that some celebrities maintain. In a story on actress Mary Tyler Moore's alcohol dependence and enrollment at the Betty Ford Center, *People* magazine reported:

> People who know Mary Tyler Moore see in her, beneath the cheery small talk and constant kindness, "an iron control," as a friend put it.
>
> "Everybody who knows her knows about the hermetic side of her, the reserve you can't burn through with an acetylene torch."

Once more with feeling

Subjects who speak with passion about their work are often quoteworthy. Here is the lead for a story by Richard Morgan in *Adweek* called "Pepsi Prez to Bottlers: We'll Slice the Competition":

> SAN FRANCISCO—"I can f-e-e-e-l the vision," said Roger Enrico, sounding more like an excited evangelist than the soft-drink company president/CEO he is. "And I can f-e-e-e-l success," continued the main man at Pepsi-Cola USA.
>
> For those still doubtful among the 2,000 bottlers, spouses and agency executives recently crowded into the Masonic Auditorium atop San Francisco's Nob Hill, Enrico then intoned the specifics:
>
> "I can f-e-e-e-l Slice becoming a 10-share brand," he said, "a 500-million-case business and . . . "—here it comes—"the third-largest trademark in the industry."

Rodney Dangerfield gets more respect than I do

Jack H. Watson, Jr., who served as President Jimmy Carter's chief of staff, told reporters that the job was often likened to that of a football quarterback, a hockey goalie, or a utility infielder, when it fact is was a thankless task:

> The image in my mind was that of a javelin catcher.

Evasive but witty

Bob Nylen, publisher of the award-winning but now-defunct *New England Monthly*, when asked if regional magazines can break away from formula journalism and still make a profit, replied:

> The answer is an unequivocal yes and no.

Smug but dim-witted

Asked Harry Warner of Warner Brothers Pictures in 1927:

> Who the hell wants to hear actors talk?

Said Grover Cleveland in 1905:

> Sensible and responsible women do not want to vote.

Said Tris Speaker in 1921:

> Ruth made a big mistake when he gave up pitching.

Here's your question right in your face

When the *Chicago Tribune* purchased the Chicago Cubs, the newspaper's management threatened to build a new stadium on 110 acres it owns in suburban Schaumburg, Illinois, and move the team there.

The Schaumburg Cubs?

Asked if this were a ploy, Cubs general manager Dallas Green said:

> I don't ploy.

The evasive put-down

Former ABC *Monday Night Football* partner Frank Gifford, whose TV work Howard Cosell criticized in his book *I Never Played the Game*, said:

> I didn't read Howard's last book, so I won't have any trouble with this one either.

Ah, sweet victory

When Coca-Cola announced that the formula for Coke was going to be changed, rival Pepsi-Cola president Roger Enrico gave Pepsi employees the day off to celebrate the "victory." Then he said with a straight face:

> Sometimes I think this is a sinister plot by Coke to keep us away from our desks and celebrating.

Expletives deleted

Ever since Richard Nixon released the transcripts of his infamously edited White House tapes, expletives have been deleted in the press as a means of getting the flavor of a good quote across with rubbing readers' noses in the unsavory particulars.

This reached a high point at the *Boston Globe* when reporters covering a Mafia racketeering trial reproduced part of a tape made by prosecutors during a poker game. At one point, sore loser Ilario M. A. Zannino angrily blamed the dealer for his bad luck and shouted a stream of 217 words, 37 of them obscenities. Part of the diatribe appeared as follows:

> [Two expletives]. You are a [two expletives]. You [expletive] punk. Get up. I don't want you here. Go home, you [expletive] rat [expletive]. Every [expletive] you made [dealt] him a [expletive] straight. You dirty rat [expletive] that you are. Get out, go home. Get the [expletive] out of here, you [expletive]. That last [expletive] card, I can't believe it.

The ironic vision

Quoting someone ironically means capturing the mood as well as the verbal particulars. This was done effectively by interviewer Nancy Collins for *Rolling Stone* when she got actor Don Johnson to talk about a long period of drug abuse before he went into a treatment program.

Johnson discussed the pernicious interplay of alcohol and cocaine:

> "I realized I could drink more if I had a little coke, and that if I had a drink it would be nice to have some coke to

go with it," said the actor. "It was a great marriage—if you wanted to vegetate."

If you can't say something nice . . . let's hear it

When a subject is under pressure and quotes his or her critics, the situation can make for lively copy. West Virginia supreme court chief justice Richard Neely, for instance, infuriated feminists when he fired his secretary for refusing to babysit.

> "They never said I was a bad judge," he said of demonstrators calling for his resignation. "They just called me a scumbag."

Taking measure

A quote that summarizes time, breadth, or depth in an interesting manner can be appealing. When Erich Segal was asked about the length of his novel *The Class* (longer than his three previous books all strung together), he said:

> This isn't a watercolor. It's a mural.

Off the record goes on the record

The request for "off the record" protection only works if it precedes the quote, not when it follows. When the latter occurs, the request becomes a scintillating part of the quote when it appears in print.

After a jury found him innocent, Claus von Bulow was disputing some of the state's theories that were raised during his second trial. For one thing, he refuted the assertion that his wife Sunny had suffered scratches in a fight with him for her life:

> "A man may—I'm not saying this is right—*slap* a woman with an open hand," he told writer Joyce Wadler for *New York* magazine. "He may even, God forbid, hit a woman with his fist. But *scratching*? That is really a rather *feminine* way of fighting, don't you agree? We *are* speaking off the record, of course."

Of course not.

Flabbergasted

One senator, evaluating the mess surrounding the Walker family on trial for spying:

> I believe it is easier to get a security clearance in the Navy than it is to get an American Express card.

Exasperated

At the beginning of the World's Worst Avid Golfer Tournament, grocer Angelo Spagnolo explained his addiction to a game that did not love him back.

> "I took up golf because my bowling was so bad," he said, "'though I didn't lose *that* many bowling balls."

(He "won" the tournament.)

If it's worth repeating, it's probably worth quoting

After firing a high school coach in football-crazy Massillon, Ohio, the president of the school board explained to *Sports Illustrated*:

> It has been extremely, extremely, I repeat, *extremely* difficult for Mike to take criticism.

As you like it

When an interviewee uses similes—that is, comparisons using the words *like* or *as*—good quotes are sure to follow.

At a Boston hearing on divorce proceedings, one woman said that after twenty-one years of divorce, her former husband had paid only $1,000 a year in child support for each of three children.

> "Going through a divorce is like being hit by a Mack truck," she said. "It knocks everybody out financially, physically and emotionally."

Talk is cheap

Accountants may run the world, but few people admire cheapskates. Accordingly, any comment on the pecuniary nature of people in the public eye is material for a good quote.

When the Detroit Tigers won the World Series in 1968, for example, the team's management decided to base the quality of players' rings on the size of the post-season share voted to each player. Pitcher Bill Scherrer, who joined the team thirty-four days before the end of the season, had his ring appraised. He learned the stone in the middle was glass, and the value was between $90 and $250.

Outfielder Kirk Gibson added the final insult:

> I've seen better rings around the collar.

Always say never

Statements of certainty, usually employing the words *always* or *never*, usually make good quotes. Boston University president John R. Silber was considered a top contender for the post of education secretary in the Reagan cabinet, particularly after he had an interview with White House counselor Edwin Meese.

When asked if he would take the job, Silber said:

> I never answer a question that has not been asked.

Quoting a sage

Hand-me-down advice, whether from a living sage or a philosopher long gone, can make for a good quote.

Here is Red Sox pitcher Dennis "Oil Can" Boyd, on what he learned from Baseball Hall of Famer Satchel Paige:

> Satchel told me, "Throw peas at their knees, high riders under their chins. Throw it there when they're lookin' here and throw it here when they're lookin' there."

Oblivious

Good quotes often come from people who are oblivious of the possible consequences of their situation. In fact, it's not a situation—it's a predicament they are in, and they are the last to know.

James Bradley, an All-American basketball player at Memphis State in 1978, left school without a diploma (he earned only 76 of 132 hours required) and without work. Not good enough to make the pros, he was interviewed, living with his mother, six years later:

> "It doesn't seem like I can get a decent job without that piece of paper," he told *USA Today* writers Kathy Blumenstock and Eric Brady in a story called "No Diplomas Awarded for Jump Shots." (Memphis State graduated only 10.7 percent of its basketball scholarship athletes.)

The story concluded with a paragraph summarizing Bradley's plight:

> "All of this makes me feel like I haven't accomplished anything." Even so, he has no regrets about playing basketball at MSU. "Life at Memphis State was real cool," he said, sitting on the front stoop of his mother's home. "I enjoyed it."

The improved adverb

When an adjective is turned into an adverb in the same sentence, grammarians may be offended, but most readers will like the resulting echolalia.

During the cola wars—when Pepsi and Coke were introducing new brands and variations—Thomas E. Ricks of the *Wall Street Journal* did a report on small soft-drink companies that were being elbowed off grocery-store shelves by the two giants' new drinks. The result:

> "The little guy is getting littler," said the publisher of a beverage industry newsletter.

Alliteration

On the death of James Beard, fellow author Richard Sax said:

> His major contribution is that he put the American
> kitchen on the map. . . . He took us from the covered wagon
> to the Cuisinart.

Repetition

After leaving her post at the United Nations, Jeanne Kirkpatrick was being pressed on whether she felt let down by President Reagan:

> "No," she replied. "No, no, no, no, no."

Ignorance

When Michelle Johnson was cast to play a role in director Stanley Donen's *Blame It on Rio*, she had no idea she'd need a passport:

> I didn't know where Rio was. I thought it was in Nevada.

Criticism

Criticism can be a great instructor, particularly when it punctures statistics that are misleading. It can also spark interest, which is what a good quote ought to do. Punter Pat McInally of the Cincinnati Bengals (who averaged forty-five yards a punt), took Ray Guy, the acclaimed Raiders punter, to task in *Sports Illustrated*:

> If Ray Guy is the model punter, he's a pretty poor model.
> He's always had a high average, but that's because he's always
> kicking the ball in the end zone from the 50-yard-line.

(Thus, Guy allows opponents to take over the ball on the 20-yard line, instead of pinning them down closer to the goal line.)

Making it seem simple

The words *simple*, *hard*, and other absolutes often trigger a good quote, if there are some particulars explaining the nature of the task.

Time magazine writers asked Jackie Gleason why *The Honeymooners* remained so appealing, for example. His reply:

> I have two answers, and they're very simple. First,
> they're funny. And second, the audiences like the people in
> *The Honeymooners*. Once you get an audience to like you,
> you're home.

Jokes

In a column on Ted Kennedy's weight problem over the years, *Boston Globe* writer Mike Barnicle at first feigned sympathy:

> Who among us cannot identify with that? Let the person
> who has never had a weight problem cast the first jelly donut.

Then he expressed amazement at the number of jokes going around:

> When Teddy is at McDonald's, you can watch the numbers
> change on the sign. . . . He cut himself shaving and gravy came
> out. . . . You know where he stands: there's a dent in the ground
> . . . . Watching Ted Kennedy get out of a chair is like watching
> the Russians get out of Afghanistan. . . . When he stands to
> speak, his shoes are in a different zip code. . . . He had to send
> out for wider laurels to rest on. . . . He got an honorary degree
> from Julia Child. . . . There's no getting around Ted Kennedy
> unless you're driving a high-mileage car. . . . He gets group rates
> from Delta Airlines. . . . Teddy's campaign slogan is, "If you can't
> stand the heat in the kitchen, eat the cookies in the living room."
> . . . He has a sign on his desk saying, "The burp stops here." . . .
> When the Republicans talk about cutting fat out of the budget,
> Teddy takes it personally.

Q stands for cute

The letter *Q* can lead to some quirky quotes. Consider, for instance, the quote from an advertising agency CEO on replacing Gilbert Gottfried as the voice of the squawking duck in a popular ad campaign for the mellow Japanese market:

> The Aflac quack is quite a quack. But for the Japanese, I'm sure a quieter quack will be quite as quirky. And that's my quick quote on that quack.

Incredulity

When a subject can't understand why others are perplexed at inappropriate behavior, the quote arises nicely from the situation:

> "I don't know why people would be so upset with accounting scandals in ad agencies. We're paid to make stuff up," said Steve Hayden of Ogilvy & Mather, talking about "creative accounting."

Vanity

Readers grow weary of humility, false and otherwise. If a subject confesses to being proud, ambitious, or vain, get ready for a good quote, provided the interviewee isn't ponderous. If there is a touch of wit and emphasis, use italics and an exclamation mark for additional effect.

Conductor Georg Solti, winner of numerous Grammys for his recordings, spoke candidly to *USA Today* on what the trophies mean to him:

> My dear, I am a vain creature. A *terribly* vain creature. *Tremendously* vain. They mean a great deal to me and I love it. I have all 23 in my studio. There are so many now that it looks like some sort of contemporary sculpture. And I *don't* like being threatened by this Mr. Michael Jackson!

Aphorisms

Singer Pearl Bailey, a judge at the Miss America Pageant, was asked about the previous year's winner, Vanessa Williams, whose reign came to a halt when *Penthouse* magazine published some old nude photos.

> "She did not know that notoriety is fame's understudy," said Bailey.

Then she quoted another master of the aphorism:

> Sophie Tucker said: "It's not how good you are, honey, it's how long you last."

Self-definitions

The looking-glass question, "Who am I?" is occasionally answered, and the result can be thunderous. Truman Capote's often-quoted self-assessment is one example:

> I'm an alcoholic. I'm a drug addict. I'm a homosexual. I'm a genius.

Single words

Ask "How would you describe the situation in a single word?" and the answer you get may be a good quote. A Texas official looked up from his bureaucratic job in the midst of a serious drought and replied:

> Disaster.

Yogi-isms

Bespeaking the obvious, with an earnest expression, can be laughable. Yogi Berra has made a small career out of it. The origins of Yogi-isms can be traced at least as far back as Yogi's manager at the New York Yankees, Casey Stengel, who once observed:

> Good pitching will always stop good hitting, and vice versa.

Humor, seemingly unintended, is the chief requirement for this type of good quote. It helps if the subject is an athlete. Pitcher Joaquin Andujar, for example, told Peter Gammons of *CNN*:

> Baseball can be summed up in one word—*youneverknow.*

Better still, it helps if the subject is Yogi Berra, who usually sounds as if he just attended a graduate seminar on the wit and wisdom of Gracie Allen.

> It ain't over 'til it's over.

While that is perhaps his most oft-quoted quote, there are many others. After attending a State Department dinner, Berra observed:

> You couldn't keep a conversation going at all. Everybody was talking too much.

As a result of Berra's reputation for hilarious quotability, almost anything that Yogi mutters is likely to turn up with quote marks around it. Here, for instance, is the lead for a *New York Times* story entitled "Berra to Be Coach in Houston":

> Yogi Berra, who in 39 major-league years as a player, manager, and coach worked only for the Yankees and the Mets, will leave home next season to serve as a coach with the Houston Astros.
> "I'm going there," Berra said yesterday.

Has Yogi ever been misquoted?

> "I really didn't say everything I said," said Yogi.

CHAPTER 15

Off the Record

How to Cut through the Confusion & Minimize the Risks

The care and handling of off-the-record information can make—or break—a story. Unnamed sources and off-the-record information are often the source of trouble, especially in the wake of the Jayson Blair scandal at the *New York Times*. Blair, you will recall, used anonymous information and fake sources, and it was the worst of *Times* for colleagues and editors there. The general practice is not to use unnamed sources, unless there is no other way to get information.

Still, any information veiled in off-the-record attribution has the irresistible aura of delicious truth. It's as though someone were to call you over and say, listen, I'm going to whisper some deep secret in your ear. Or perhaps a dark secret slips out . . . and you try to take it back, but you can't. You can only hope that when that information is revealed, your name will not be associated with it. President George W. Bush, for example, has been known to put his hands around a reporter's ears for an "off record" declaration after the fact . . . as in, you didn't hear that . . . right?

Well, yes . . . and no. "Off the record" is such an ambiguous term.

Many publications have strict rules for the use of anonymous sources—the disclosure of their identities to editors, for instance, who can then corroborate the information. When anonymous sources are used, attributions need to be as specific as possible, such as "according to a state official familiar with the budget process." Writers often have to juggle options, deciding between the public interest and private fears, between the need for a lively story and the need for documentation.

Sometimes there is an obvious need for off-the-record protection: a cop whose information is vital to a story, but who cannot release his name without penalty; or a claim by someone who is blowing the whistle on his company, but who wants total anonymity.

Be aware of how far your editor can go to back you up and guarantee that any promises of anonymity are maintained at all levels. A chill was sent through the ranks of off-the-record sources when a Minneapolis court awarded $700,000 to a man whose identity was revealed after he had been promised anonymity by the *Minneapolis Star Tribune* in 1988. In the coverage of this case, it became evident that while reporters almost without exception honor their promises of anonymity, they find it increasingly difficult to do so without first consulting their editor, who in turn may have to check it out with higher-ups, including the legal department.

"Thus it becomes even more likely that the source's name will be mentioned," noted one PR agent. "Law suits are increasingly common. When an aggrieved person or institution sues, they'll go beyond the news organization and include the source, named or eventually to be named."

Legal and PR firms urge clients not to be off-the-record sources for stories. It's too risky and leaves them open to the possibility of litigation.

A hypothetical example

Let's assume you are working on a story about unethical practices in the publishing industry, and I am one of your key sources.

- During one of our interviews I tell you—off the record—that I once knew a literary agent who used his well-known clients, including a bestselling novelist, as a front to collect "reading fees" from numerous unsuspecting beginning writers who were invited to submit their manuscripts to this agency for an "evaluation." Would you be able to use the information?

- If, in another interview, I tell you—off the record—that a certain publisher was conducting a writing competition, with very modest cash prizes, while making a considerable profit from thousands of entry fees, would you be able to use the information?

• If I tell you—again, strictly off the record—that after submitting my manuscript to that agent (with a $600 check for a critique), and then sending the same manuscript to the publisher's competition (with a $45 entry fee), and winning nada, I murdered the agent, then blew up the publisher's editorial offices, would you be able to use the information?

It all depends on how you define "off the record." If it means that the information is given explicitly for your knowledge only—and is not to be printed or made public in any way—and furthermore that the information cannot to be taken to another source to get official confirmation, then you, as a writer, are all dressed up with nowhere to go.

We are being hypothetical here, of course, but a real-life version of this dilemma turned up in a notorious case recently, when a private investigator named Len Jenoff tearfully told Nancy Phillips, a reporter for the *Philadelphia Inquirer*, that he arranged the murder of Carol Neulander at the request of her husband, Rabbi Fred Neulander.

Phillips had cultivated Jenoff as a source, meeting him over meals, talking on the phone, pushing him to talk about his secrets while allowing him to speak "off the record." There's the rub.

"He would not give me permission to tell the story and because I had agreed to keep his confidence, I had to honor that and could not tell the authorities," Phillips wrote. "I wanted Jenoff to keep talking to me, with the hope that I could persuade him to go on the record."

Eventually, Phillips arranged for Jenoff to confess to authorities; but, until there was a confession (which ran eighty-nine pages) for the arresting officers, the information that Phillips had gained "off the record" was like handcuffs on the reporter.

Defining "off the record"

Does "off the record" always have to be so restrictive? As noted, it all depends on how you define the term. There is so much confusion over what "off the record" means that when *Folio:* ("the magazine of magazine management") asked an array of editors in 1991 to define it, there was no consensus. Here is a sampling of their replies, which demonstrates how ambiguous the term is:

> It means you can't quote the person directly. If it's an important bit of information, we'd probably suggest it in the piece.
>
> *—Zone Magazine*

> It means the person shouldn't be quoted. File away the information and try to get more on it from other sources.
>
> *—Seafood Business*

> The information is to be used only to enhance your understanding of where to go reportorially.
>
> *—Mother Jones*

> If somebody tells me something is off the record, I do not run it—but I will ask to run it without attribution.
>
> *—Travel Agent*

Perhaps the most helpful response to *Folio:*'s question was expressed by Kenneth T. Walsh, a senior writer at *U.S. News & World Report*.

"I'd always clarify with the source what he means by 'off the record,'" he said. "It can mean just his name, or the information itself."

The importance of a full and complete understanding of the term by both parties has not been lost in the courts, where a confidentiality pledge is viewed as a legally enforceable promise. In 1991 Dan Cohen was awarded $200,000 when the U.S. Supreme Court ruled against the *St. Paul Pioneer Press* and the *Minneapolis Star Tribune* for revealing his name as a source in a political story after he had been promised anonymity.

Writers should tread carefully when using off-the-record reporting techniques, which is usually how we obtain the best information in an interview. This is especially true if the topic is even mildly investigative.

When I was working on a biography of Lee Atwater, the controversial Republican political operative, at least half of the four hundred interviews I conducted were off the record. Before conducting each interview, however, I made it clear that I defined "off the record" as "not for attribution to the source," but that I would remain free to verify the information elsewhere and try to bring the information into the story from other sources.

Information gathered this way is also called "for background only," meaning anything that is said in the interview is usable, but not in direct quotation and not for attribution. The writer writes it on his own.

Just make very certain that you get the story right, and be prepared to defend yourself in court, if necessary. For the Atwater book, often I heard the same story from several sources—all off the record. Then I had to decide whether to use the material from my own perspective as consensus reportage. In some cases, I did; in others, I backed off. As you get deeper and deeper into reporting a story, you develop a sense of situational ethics, and you will know when it is right to write.

Of course, it is doubly important to verify off-the-record information before you use it to vilify someone in print. Feisty columnist Margery Eagan of the *Boston Herald* was highly critical of WHDH-TV (Channel 7) owner Ed Ansin's role in the decision not to renew anchor Kim Carrigan's contract. Eagan wrote that Ansin had been "described by employees as a despicable, ruthless, egomaniacal, power-mad narcissistic troll in need of psychoanalytic intervention." No sugar-coating there, to be sure.

Ansin's attorney called the column "nothing short of an unfounded personal attack," adding that the author, Eagan, had launched the "highly charged, personal invectives at Mr. Ansin" based in part on "unidentified 'sources' at Channel 7."

"The only thing you can do in this circumstance is file a lawsuit," Ansin told media columnist Mark Jurkowitz of the *Boston Globe*. "It's something I feel I have to do."

The case went nowhere. Was columnist Eagan guilty of libel? The legal distinction between libel and slander is not without some complications. Libel applies to written statements, slander to verbal statements and gestures. Statements made in a broadcast, however, may become part of the script, which then can reach a vast audience in written form. The question of whether broadcasts are libel or slander is often determined in the United States by individual state laws.

Should you avoid all off-the-record information?

By now, you may be thinking, *hmmm*, maybe I should just stay away from off-the-record information, and instead explain at the beginning of each interview that *nothing* is off the record. That way, if a source doesn't want to say something, he should refrain from commenting. Then, if he calls the boss "a power-mad narcissistic troll in need of psychoanalytic intervention," I've got a lively quote on the record and a source for attribution.

While this is certainly a safer approach, it is also rigid and may affect the rapport you are trying to establish at the outset of an interview. Moreover, because so many good stories—even confessions—are heard, initially, off the record, you may never know about the big ones that got away.

Tips and tactics

For those of you who want to hear the good, the bad, even the ugly, here are seven steps for using "off the record" to your advantage:

1. **Agree on what "off the record" means at the beginning of the interview.**

Don't wait until it comes up midway through your conversation or, far worse, right after you have heard a juicy story. Your basic choices for definition include the following:

- Not to be used in any way.

- Use for background only.

- Not for attribution (that is, you can use the information, but don't attribute it to the subject).

- Use, but attribute to "a source close to the chairman" or some anonymous source.

- Use only if you can verify the information from another source; then use that latter subject as the source for attribution in the story.

By defining the term in advance (and the last two definitions best serve the needs of the writer), you will avoid the self-editing subject who gives good quotes, then says, "Uh, that was off the record."

2. Define it in a way that you are not handcuffed by the information.

Put the source at ease with your methodology: "If you want to go off the record, tell me in advance and I will not attribute the information to you—but I may find it elsewhere, or I may even have the information from another source as we speak. In any case, there will be no fingerprints linking the information to you."

3. Make it clear that the subject is the one who needs to take action to put information off the record.

If you are using a tape recorder, point to the "off" button and instruct the subject: "Hit this button if you are going off the record. Then I will know that everything on the tape is on the record."

4. If something does come up, don't be too quick to offer to let the subject off the hook.

You can assume that information is on the record—unless there is a clear agreement or understanding that it is not. It may be better to apologize afterward than to ask permission in advance. Subjects do not admire the obsequious interviewer. Be direct, even assertive.

In a study of questions used by reporters, it was found that "Do you mind if I quote you?" was less productive than a more assertive approach, such as "That's fine. I'll quote you on that."

5. Verify all off-the-record information before using it in your story.

Some sources will hide behind "off the record" to slam others or to promote their own personal agendas. Don't be fooled.

6. When in doubt, do without.

If the off-the-record information cannot be confirmed, remember the old newsroom axiom, "Sometimes it's better to kill a story than to be killed by a story."

7. Protect your sources.

If a confidential source gives you helpful information that makes the story, mum's the word when lawyers call. According to the *American Journalism Review*, your promise is backed in varying degrees by "shield laws" in thirty states and the District of Columbia.

Regardless, do the right thing—and be prepared to go directly to jail, if the situation comes to that.

CHAPTER 16

Liar, Liar, Interviews Afire

How to Keep Your Story Accurate

In the interviewing trade, there are lies, damned lies, and publicity tours. Subjects going through hard times will often engage in denial for their public audience. Of course, tabloids thrive on half-truths and innuendo, but even the serious press was fooled by actor Tom Cruise, who appeared on the covers of nearly every major magazine in a promotional blitz for the release of *Born on the Fourth of July*.

Regarding his then-marriage to actress Mimi Rogers, Cruise told *Time*: "The most important thing for me is I want Mimi to be happy." Two weeks later he told *Rolling Stone*: "I couldn't imagine being without her or being alone." Ten days later he told *Us* magazine: "I just really enjoy our marriage."

The following week the couple announced they were getting a divorce.

"Who said that the tabloids are always wrong and that serious magazines are always right?" observed *Newsweek*. "And furthermore, who ever said Tom Cruise always tells the truth?"

For veterans of the interviewing wars, lying is indeed often a cat-and-mouse game. A *New Yorker* cartoon by Arny Lewin depicts a businessman sitting in his lawyer's office as the lawyer says, "Okay—let's review what you didn't know and when you didn't know it."

Former New York City mayor Ed Koch, for instance, was known to withhold key facts when answering questions. Once, when asked about a particular discrepancy, Koch replied: "If you ask me the question and you ask it sufficiently pointedly, you will get an accurate response." In other words: "I am not required to tell you everything I know." Indeed, for many interviewees, the truth is not necessarily the whole truth, and lying to interviewers is perfectly okay—unless they are caught. Then they will gladly explain why it's entirely your fault for asking the question the wrong way.

We live in an age in which scarcely a month goes by without a clergyman being defrocked, a politician being debunked, or a hero being knocked off his or her pedestal. It would be pleasant if everyone's background were impeccable, but unfortunately this is rarely the case. One executive search firm has estimated that at least 50 percent of all job applicants "feel the need to embellish the facts."

The Liars Index, a study conducted every six months by executive search firm Werra & Associates, found that 11 percent of upper-management applicants lied on their resumes in 2002; this was down from a remarkable 23 percent in early 2000. (In any study about lying, of course, one has to wonder if the respondents are telling the truth.) The most common credential lie involves educational background—where *BS* may mean something altogether different. This is probably true of interview subjects as well.

Subjects sometimes lie, or call it "fibbing," just for the fun of it. Supermodel Suzy Parker loved to give reporters a hard time, often opening an interview by pointing out that the initials of her real name—Cecilia Rene Ann Park—form a word that has been used to describe her way with the truth. Over the years she told interviewers that she was born in Texas (of a poor family), in Virginia (of a first family), and in Florida (of a bourgeois family).

"I always tell the truth," she explained, "but today's truth might not be tomorrow's."

For his book *The Hustons*, Lawrence Grobel interviewed hundreds of people who knew and worked with John Huston. "During the many hours of talking to these and other people, it soon became clear that memories weren't always the same, that events witnessed by three or more people were often seen in three or more ways."

Grobel didn't believe that anyone was falsifying accounts. "Everyone told the truth as he or she saw or remembered it."

Is it the interviewer's goal to catch a subject in repose? Or in a lie? As a reporter, you are expected to be like a camera, getting photographs that are candid, whereas the subject would like you to leave with perfectly posed portraits that can be generously retouched, if the subject so desires. Within a short period of time, with little more than personality and a tape recorder, the interviewer is expected to get the subject to shed his or her inhibitions.

This is not easily done. While it's pretty to think that trust is what is at the foundation of human relations, the simple truth is that people lie. Some people clearly lie because they believe there is a good reason or greater benefit, in their eyes, to be deceptive. Others may lie simply for the pure enjoyment of hiding the truth, enjoying the game as much as the outcome.

In either case, while lying is something an interviewer wants to ferret out, discovering that someone is in fact lying can make a story more colorful.

"If someone lies to me in front of my camera, I think that's interesting," says master photographer Richard Avedon. "I think a person who's lying is really interesting, much more interesting than some bore who tells the truth."

One neuropsychologist claims he can tell how stressed a person is by how often the person blinks. A "normal" rate for someone speaking on camera is 30 to 50 blinks per minute. More than 50 bpm is "high," according to Boston College neuropsychologist Joe Tecce. Someone hitting 70 bpm is high on the stress chart, but not frantic.

Watching a CNN interview with Saddam Hussein, Tecce measured the Iraqi dictator blinking as often as 123 times per minute, which likely made him the most tense player in the recent war.

"Really good liars," however, do not "fidget, stammer, [or] avoid eye contact," noted one human resource consultant in *Fortune* magazine.

How to keep your story accurate

There are several ways for untruths to get into an interview and then into a published story. First, too many interviewers do not take the time to check a fact. Instead, they go with their "gut instinct," based mostly on the rapport established during the interview process. A subject who performs well in an interview is considered reliable, believable. But clearly this "halo factor" precludes the objective evaluation of the actual facts involved. Coolness by the subject during the interview can be deceptive.

Plain old fact-checking tends to work best to spot dishonesty. If someone says he graduated from Harvard, it's easy to check whether Harvard has ever heard of him. To do a background check on work performance, phone previous bosses, colleagues, and subordinates.

For a *New York* magazine feature on stress-testing (a procedure recommended for people whose medical histories show them to be at high risk for heart disease), medical reporter Martha Hume visited several of New York's better-known "health spas," where she found many incorrect and some dangerous practices, including the absence of a qualified physician during the test. At one spa, Hume interviewed a Dr. Maxim Asa, a poseur who had neither an M.D. nor the Ph.D. he claimed.

Hume became suspicious when a staffer who had been introduced to her as being the cardiologist who would monitor her test turned out to be the same man who had been introduced to her the week before as an "exercise physiologist." After paying $350 for a procedure that "included many tests designed for show rather than out of necessity," Hume decided that the spa required closer investigation.

She called Asa to get the names of the two "on-staff" cardiologists he had told her about. She checked their names in the *Directory of Medical Specialists*, which lists the names and credentials of all board-certified medical specialists in the United States, but found neither was listed as a specialist in cardiovascular disease.

Dr. Asa had also told the writer that he held a Ph.D. in exercise physiology from "Springfield University" in Massachusetts. Hume found that there was a Springfield College in that state. A representative of the registrar's office there confirmed that a Mordechai Maxim Asa had earned a master of physical education degree, but there was no record of him having earned a Ph.D.

The writer's conclusion can be summarized in the article's title: "Warning: It has been determined that a stress test can be dangerous to your health."

To identify sources able to double-check facts or perspectives, you might even ask the subject during an interview if there is one person with whom she or he did not get along. Afterward, go to the phone to check out the differences of opinion. In doing phone checks, accentuate the negative.

"If you could suggest one area for improvement in Bill, what might it be?" is a common technique used in checking references for job interviews. This usually gets to the negative heart of the matter, if there is one to be explored.

Interview techniques to avoid being lied to

During an interview, it is advisable to assume the demeanor of a private eye. "In my business, you have to buy everybody's act," says the protagonist in James Crumbley's splendid murder mystery, *The Last Good Kiss*. "For a few minutes."

Or consider yourself a border guard. Scrutinize, appraise a subject's story and body language, and wave him through—or direct him off to the side for further questioning.

A lot of what you do is just common sense. Look for things that are out of place, a story that doesn't make sense. If he's evasive or won't look you right in the eye, make a note and follow up later.

Always pause after an answer. Don't move on until you have received a full reply. Explore each answer fully before moving on to your next questions. Never assume that a subject is giving you all she has in one quote-worthy burst.

When it comes to numbers, act like an accountant doing a tax return: insist on documentation. A reporter for the *Boston Globe* rather naively accepted inaccurate statistics from his sources and wrote a story called "Endangered: Black Men" in which he reported that "three black men die for every white man." The article also claimed: "In 1984–86 alone, homicide claimed the lives of 903.6 young black men per 100,000."

The errors were so staggering that a statistician counted six numerical errors, three ambiguities, and a typo in an article that depended absolutely on numerical accuracy. Even if the murder rate were 300 per 100,000, for instance, then about 28,000 black men would have been murdered in one of those years—a figure that is more than the number of all people who were murdered in this country (about 20,000).

"I have seen mistakes like these in articles about working mothers, black professional women, candy manufacturing, prison demographics, railroad-station construction, and elsewhere in the paper," wrote one careful reader. "The trouble seems to be worse when writers used to 'soft' or sociological articles have to deal with unfamiliar numbers. They swallow them, and the editors let them."

Be on the guard for glib braggadocio as well. Bill Heater was the writer and the voice behind those carless (some would say careless) Infiniti "Zen" ads that featured seascapes, landscapes, but no automobiles on camera. In an interview, he told a writer working on a *Boston Magazine* story, "We really felt that what we were selling wasn't the exterior or skin of the car as much as the spirit of the car. The car in a lot of ways is a cultural statement, an expression of Japanese culture. We felt we should focus on aspects of that culture, such as the harmony between man and nature that you see in the commercials."

Okay, so much for the PR fluff. Now, the interviewer probed: "Are the ads working?"

"They're doing a tremendous amount of business," Heater replied. "Whether that can be attributed to the advertising or the fact that the car has been well received in the motor press, I don't know."

That sounds like a PR response, don't you think? Unfortunately, the reporter had no follow-up question to probe into the brag that the ads were working, or to insist on a statistical pinning-down of that "tremendous amount of business" boast. Instead, the next question the reporter asked was, "Have you done any other voice-overs?"

While Heater was handling that softball question, *Adweek* magazine was reporting that seven weeks into the launch of the Infiniti, Nissan Motor Corporation had a huge problem on its hands. The ad campaign with its Zen-like focus on nature and total aversion to car shots had analysts questioning, competitors laughing, and Infiniti dealers grousing loudly: they were most assuredly *not* doing a tremendous amount of business.

How many cars had been sold since the ads began? Infiniti executives had steadfastly refused to discuss numbers, but, after some prodding, the magazine found that only 1,700 cars had been sold since the launch.

And Bill Heater? He left the ad agency to work on a screenplay.

Reflecting on his early years as a writer, John Gregory Dunne once observed that he had a mentor, a "D.I. of my intellectual boot camp. He taught me to accept nothing at face value, to question everything, above all to be wary."

That's the stuff that tough interviewing is made of.

And that's no lie.

CHAPTER 17

The PRoblem with PR

Jeffrey Toobin, trying to interview Martha Stewart for a *New Yorker* profile, hit a stone wall as the stylish marketer came under investigation for insider trading of ImClone stock. "As unpleasant as the insider-trading investigation has been," wrote Toobin, "the coverage by the press— a cascade of ridicule and abuse—may have been harder to take." This appeared to be especially true for Martha's PR advisers, who said no when Toobin came to call.

Then, as things really heated up in Martha's kitchen—comic Conan O'Brien quoted Stewart as saying "a subpoena should be served with a nice appetizer"—the PR wall began to collapse. Frustrated by the bad publicity, Martha's advisers "saw that there might be advantages for their client in such an interview," said Toobin. Martha wouldn't speak on the record about the facts of the case, but she would "discuss her feelings about the investigation, and the public reaction."

So it came to pass that on a Sunday afternoon in Connecticut, Toobin and Stewart walked around her house, amidst Chow Chow dogs and Himalayan cats (named Teeny, Weeny, Mozart, Verdi, Vivaldi, Berlioz, and Bartok) and listening to the screech of some thirty American song canaries. They settled in at the dining-room table, where Martha had lined up three pens, an unlined white writing pad that matched her pens, and all of her advisers for the interview.

Toobin noticed that, suddenly, his subject looked weary.

"*Schadenfreude?*" he inquired.

"That's the word," replied Martha. "I hear that, like, every day." It was just empathetic enough to launch the interview in a casual, sympathetic, yet sophisticated manner.

Then, ever the precisionist, she inquired, "Do you know how to spell it?"

They were off and babbling, almost oblivious to the chaperone-like presence of Martha's advisers, with whom Toobin had needed to deal to make the interview happen.

Webster defines *symbiosis* as "the intimate living together of two dissimilar organisms in a mutually beneficial relationship." Some would say that it is the appropriate description of the relationship between a PR person and a journalist. Increasingly, for the interviewer today, PR is the first word in press.

In a scene from Michael Moore's documentary film *The Big One*, the director is talking to Nike CEO Phil Knight about labor conditions at the sneaker factories in Indonesia. "Twelve-year-olds working in factories," says Moore. "That's okay with you?"

"They're not twelve-year-olds working in factories," says Knight. "The minimum age is fourteen."

"How about fourteen, then?" asks Moore. "Doesn't that bother you?"

"No."

When word drifted back to Nike central, PR spokesman Lee Weinstein met with Moore to discuss damage control. Nike and Weinstein had two problems with the interview, observed Garry Trudeau in an essay for *Time* magazine.

"First, it was unfair to include Knight's endorsement of a 14-year-old labor force while leaving out his subsequent pledge to make a transition to 16-year-olds (a difficult task, says Nike, given the workers' propensity for using 'forged documents'). Second, Knight referred to his employees as 'poor little Indonesian workers,' a characterization that failed to convey the respect in which he held them. In both instances, Weinstein insisted, Phil had 'misspoken.' What would it take to make these two classic moments go away?"

Well, now. The populist filmmaker said he couldn't remove anything from the movie, but if Nike were to build a facility in Flint, Michigan, he would add a new scene. Weinstein, heartened, whipped out a notepad.

"Would that be a shoe factory or a warehouse?"

"Anything that'll employ 500 people at a livable wage," said Moore, barely keeping a straight face.

Weinstein promised to get back to him. Moore is still waiting.

George Orwell had it about right when he said that journalism is printing what someone else does not want printed; everything else is public relations. Today, life in the quid pro quo world of arranging interviews and maintaining control of the story is increasingly difficult for the writer in what has been called the Age of Contrivance. "Two centuries ago when a great man appeared, people looked for God's purpose in him," wrote Daniel Boorstin in *The Image: A Guide to Pseudo-Events in America.* "Today we look for his press agent."

Everybody has one. Take PFC Jessica Lynch, for example. After her ordeal as a prisoner of war for ten days in the Iraqi War, her family was swamped with film offers. A press agent was soon coordinating a book and movie deal.

This was a modest undertaking compared to the deal-making coordinated by the parents of former kidnapping victim Elizabeth Smart. A generation ago, the Smarts might have turned to a confessor or a psychologist in their time of stress, observed Daniel Henninger in the *Wall Street Journal.* But at today's "Code Red level of temporary fame," Elizabeth's parents hired not one, but two PR representatives to oversee a movie deal and other marketing opportunities.

A pseudo-event, observes Boorstin, is a synthetic occurrence that makes up for the lack of spontaneous events—thus, the Photo Opportunity, or the Interview with more ground rules than a game of donkey baseball. Everything is processed and homogenized for public consumption.

As far back as 1980, the *Columbia Journalism Review* looked at one issue of the *Wall Street Journal* and found that 45 percent of the news that day was taken from press handouts: thirty-two press releases were printed almost verbatim, while twenty-one others contained only perfunctory additional reporting.

Since then, the public relations industry has become the de facto assignment editor for much of the content of American newspapers. When architectural writer Robert Campbell saw an ad in the *New York Times* for a building called The Corinthian, he was intrigued by the notion of a towerlike structure with suburban overtones in midtown Manhattan. He tried to set up an interview with the principals.

"I called the Corinthian's leasing agent, who referred me to the developer, who referred me to the owner, who referred me to the public relations consultant, who sent me a large pile of lush prose."

Lush prose, it seems, is the preferred style of reporting in PR circles. Lush prose—and control.

Consider what author and *Forbes FYI* editor Christopher Buckley went through while trying to line up interviews for a story on Frank Sinatra at Caesars Palace in Las Vegas.

Buckley knew from the start—courtesy of Sinatra's PR man in New York, who informed Buckley that the only thing he couldn't do for him was to "arrange an interview with the man"—that the piece would, of necessity, be an Impression of a Scene. So Buckley figured the best way to research the story would be to "try to get close to those who are close to Himself." The only people who would give Christopher Buckley the time of day were the Caesars Palace employees.

The writer's working methods were varied. One night he even tried to bribe Harry the valet to exchange clothes with Buckley and let the writer take Sinatra his freshly pressed chemise. Harry's eyes dilated at the sight of a fifty-dollar bill, but no, he would surely lose his job and he had a kid going to college in the East.

From there, it was back to a rum and coke at the Caesars Palace bar where Buckley planned more strategies for getting interviews. First stop was Jim Mahoney, Sinatra's PR man in Vegas, who proceeded to avoid Buckley for two days. One night, after the writer followed him very conspicuously from the poker table to the baccarat table to the blackjack table, Mahoney consented to talk.

Buckley was playing it very low key—"Mr. Mahoney" this, "Mr. Mahoney" that. Finally, over a beer, Mahoney said, "Suppose you give me one good reason I should cooperate with you on this story." Buckley replied that, the sins of the press notwithstanding, he was not out there to "screw" Sinatra. He was only interested in his emotion vis-à-vis another Las Vegas engagement.

After two hours of nothing but Sinatra encomiums—"He still sends this tingly feeling down my spine. Always has." *Zzzzzz.* Mahoney finally told Buckley that the only reason he was speaking to him this night was "because when I was your age, I needed someone to say, 'Hey you, kid, come over here.'"

"He was patronizing, uninformative, oddly likeable," recalls Buckley, "but I was no closer to Sinatra than I had been when I first got the call from New York."

Next stop: Ella Fitzgerald. The writer called the singer's room. "Hello, Miss Fitzgerald, my name is Christopher Buckley, and I'm here doing a piece on the show, and I was wondering if you might be able to spare me ten minutes or so for an interview."

"What are you going to ask me?" said the singer.

"Well, I thought we could talk about, you know, the mechanics of the show, how you think it's going, what it's like to perform with Mr. Sinatra . . . things like that."

"How come you want to know these things?"

Buckley was taken a little aback. "I'd just like to have an idea of, say, what goes on in your mind during one of these huge nightclub acts, you know, what's wrong with them, what's right with them."

"Well, I just don't know why you want to talk with me." This was not a "Gee-whiz, me?" reaction. Ella Fitzgerald was serious.

"Well, honestly, Miss Fitzgerald, I can't believe you don't know why I'd want to speak to you," said Buckley.

Pause.

"I don't like your attitude," replied Fitzgerald. "You call me up and get snotty. I don't like your attitude. You ask me for a favor and get snotty . . ."

Buckley tried to reiterate his good intentions, saying he was sorry if he'd offended the singer, "But, honestly, why are you so surprised I want to speak with you?"

"Well, I'll have to think about it."

"Ah, well then, shall I call you later or—"

"Goodbye."

"But—"

"Goodbye."

Two days later, Ella Fitzgerald's press agent called Buckley and said that Ella would give him fifteen minutes. "If you get her talking about her new album, she might go longer." Buckley's strategy was to start with more or less banal questions, and then to use follow-up to gather some insights into Sinatra. Of course, he would not give Fitzgerald the impression that the article was on Sinatra alone.

So Ella and Buckley finally got together, but, alas, she did not sing for him.

"Tell me, what's it like when you're playing with someone as big as Sinatra? Do you ever get the feeling the crowd is just waiting for him to come on?"

"No."

"Okay, then, but could you tell me how the show was arranged. I mean, did Sinatra's men approach you, or what?"

"I don't know. I don't do no business."

And so it beat on, a conversation to nowhere. Ella was hot because her air conditioning broke down. Buckley fixed it, said goodbye, and left.

"I'm like a marriage counselor," publicist Peggy Siegal told journalist Jenifer Conlin over a glass of wine in New York City. "Every encounter between the press and one of my clients is a potentially bad blind date.

"I spend my life trying to prevent disaster," she explained. "The trick is to know the personalities behind the editors and writers at each publication and carefully match the right stories and writers with the right clients."

Before agreeing to an interview, Siegal reads a writer's clips and tries to decide whether the writer will be sympathetic. She explains that while the job of the publicist is to "try to exercise damage control," once an interview is underway, it's strictly one on one.

"You can try to control access and have an impact on the nature of the piece, but once the client and the reporter are together, there is nothing I can do."

Well, not exactly. When a magazine writer did an unflattering article on actor Richard Gere, Siegal was able to kill the story about her client by flying with the actor to the editor's house and granting a new interview.

The name of the game is access. Magazines often compete for access to key subjects and stories. "The power of the publicist is an increasing problem for editors," observed *GQ*'s legendary editor Art Cooper. "You don't see that many nasty profiles of people in entertainment because you run the risk of losing access to that publicist's clients."

Indeed, PR staffers are often trained journalists. They graduated from the same journalism schools as editors—if the editor graduated at all. Journalism schools are not training the majority of journalists in the profession; rather, they are training PR flacks, who learn journalists' skills in order to make end runs around the process of reporting and shaping the stories that appear in the press. They know that magazines have to compete for access to key subjects and stories, and that editors, often overworked and understaffed, are under pressure to get interviews and cover stories.

Critic Louis Menand, reflecting on an earlier age when the relationship between PR and journalism was unstable, says that "Today, the marriage has been made, and though they're always picking on each other, the couple couldn't be happier."

In fact, the marriage has destabilized the area of sports and entertainment reporting, where writers in the field often end up as co-authors of autobiographies of the stars; where someone like Barbara Walters has been turned into a schmoozer with the stars. "Who in contemporary journalism would cross a celebrity?" asks Menand.

Menand answers his own question: "Contemporary journalists are too busy figuring out how to become celebrities themselves."

A good PR person is like a diplomat for the company line. One is reminded of legendary editor Caskie Stinnett's definition: "A diplomat is a person who can tell you to go to hell in such a way that you actually look forward to the trip."

They even have their own language, Flackspeak. Consider this press release on a product called Spare the Ribs, a boneless, all-meat version of "ribs" in barbecue sauce, designed to be cooked in a microwave oven. The spokesperson for Designer Foods Inc. of Wilmington, Delaware, said that a "patented Texturite process" was developed by the company "to intertwine fibers of low-cost irregular cuts of meat into products that replicate the taste and texture of natural meat muscle."

Yum. Translation: emulsified low-grade meat parts are being pressed into little rib-like shapes for lazy diners. (One version was chicken.)

Consider how spokeswoman Diane McNulty explained why *Long Island Newsday* cut five business-side employees: "In light of our rapid growth, we're placing strong emphasis on operating efficiency."

Ah, yes.

And how does flackwriting work?

"Direct quotations are a problem in organizations, whether they appear in internal publications, news releases, or speeches," said the late Lawrence Ragan, publisher of newsletters for "organizational communicators."

"Writers must decide on how accurate they will be when they quote others who work for the same organization. Their job is different from the newspaper reporter whose job and reputation depend upon absolute accuracy."

Writing in *The Bottom Line Communicator*, Ragan recalled working with a plant manager who, when angered by assembly-line employees, would roar at his subordinates, "They're pissing in your face, but you think it's rain."

Yet when Ragan had pencil in hand to quote him for a story in the plant paper, the manager's words came out like this: "Our dedicated employees, so tireless, so loyal, so committed to the purpose entrusted to them, have never let us down when we have called upon them to go the extra mile."

"Actually, he didn't speak those words," added Ragan. "I wrote them, and he liked them."

Do organizational communicators ever quote accurately? "They must find the words that express the best in the people they are quoting," according to Ragan. "If they do so skillfully, they will advance the fortunes of the organization and at the same time be faithful to the deeper meaning of its message."

By fooling with nearly all of the quotes all of the time, of course, the good little corporate communicator can advance his or her good fortune as well. Is this journalism? In a word: no. It is corporate gamesmanship, using the traditional tools of the journalist to do a sell job on the public.

Quotes are often the result of ghostwriters, who place them in an orator's mouth, from whence they are passed on to history. And yet, we remember them as the words of great orators and political leaders. White House speechwriters Raymond Moley and Louis Howe are largely forgotten today, while Franklin D. Roosevelt is remembered for mouthing their words: "The only thing we have to fear is fear itself."

Theodore Sorensen paraphrased Henry Thoreau while drafting John F. Kennedy's inaugural address, mostly remembered for "Ask not what your country can do for you, ask what you can do for your country."

Peggy Noonan defined the presidency of George H. W. Bush with words like "a thousand points of light" and "a kinder, gentler nation."

Speechwriters today, of course, are not so shy about claiming authorship. White House spokesman Larry Speakes, in *Speaking Out*, a book he wrote (cough) with Robert Pack, tells how he fabricated quotes for President Ronald Reagan and fed them to the press. When Reagan met Soviet leader Mikhail S. Gorbachev in Geneva, Speakes noted that Gorbachev had made several quotable statements about Soviet desires for peace, while Reagan said little—and was losing the public-relations battle.

Speakes instructed a press aide "to draft some quotes for the president. I polished the quotes and told the press that, while the two leaders stood together at the end of one session, the president said to Gorbachev: 'There is much that divides us, but I believe the world breathes easier because we are talking here together.'"

After his book was published to considerable media outrage over the manufactured quotes, Speakes said that making up presidential quotes "is not lying. . . . When you're a press secretary, you develop a bond of under-standing with the president so that you think like the president. . . . I knew those quotes were the way he felt."

In his book, Speakes added, "Luckily, the Russians did not dispute the quotes, and I had been able to spruce up the president's image by taking a bit of liberty with my PR man's license."

Poetic license is one thing, but PR man's license? Cleaning up quotes, matching subject and verb, and similar light copyediting is understandable, even helpful. But making up quotes and admitting it in public—this is very poor PR, indeed. "For a man in the public relations business, a man who makes his living courting the media, this book was kamikaze," observed syndicated columnist Eleanor Randolph.

Unfortunately for Larry Speakes, his admissions in *Speaking Out* (a book that he wrote while working as vice president of communications for Merrill Lynch) had violated the PR community's first commandment: be believable.

There are disquieting signs that the working press has accepted, even sought out, the "spin-meister" who will give a sharper twist, "a more pointed and quotable quote, on any development than the candidate himself is ready to utter," wrote columnist David S. Broder in the wake of the Speakes debacle. "These managers and media manipulators have achieved a certain legitimacy and status of their own, simply by giving a 'good quote' to the ever-accepting reporters." The problem does not lie with the ministry of propaganda, however. Speakes confessed to a practice that was the culmination of years of increasingly manipulative PR practices in the White House.

During the Persian Gulf war, journalists operated with one hand tied behind their collective back. Information was obtained from interviews conducted under military escort. They were told by Pentagon flacks during sanitized updates that U.S. warplanes were "degrading" (i.e., killing) the Iraqi enemy, with some "collateral damage" (destruction of nonmilitary facilities or civilian deaths).

What sort of evidence were the reporters offered? In response to a question at a press briefing, Pete Williams, assistant secretary of defense for public affairs, replied: "We just don't discuss that capability. I can't tell you why we don't discuss it, because then I'd be discussing it."

"Trust me," said Colin Powell, chairman of the joint chiefs of staff, during one briefing.

On such projects, it is nearly impossible to separate fabrication from fact. PR communicators engage in a thousand points of hype so that you see things their way—so that the judgment is favorable, even fawning if possible. While public relations springs from a basic human tendency to put the best face on things, the role of the journalist ought to be: trust no one.

Public relations began to assume its present form in 1904 when a newspaperman named Ivy Lee opened a publicity office in New York City. He became known as the father of PR because, in an era of "the public be damned," he maintained that if business would tell its side of the story, public suspicion would be dissipated. Clients included the Rockefellers, who hired him to deal with the aftermath of the infamous wholesale shooting of striking workers at a family-owned coal company in Colorado.

Another self-proclaimed "father" of PR was Edward Bernays, who invented the concept of "the engineering of consent." He gave the influence industry an academic veneer (Sigmund Freud was his uncle) and a sense of ideology that has been the motivation for many a flack trying to deliver the public to a client by way of creating a nonevent to publicize many a non-idea. Bernays began to pop up as a director of various campaigns, including the effort to get women to smoke cigarettes.

It is not clear at what point in time the field of public relations took on the hallowed status it seems to have in some quarters today. The Public Relations Society of America has 16,000 members and views Edward Bernays as no less important to its profession than Pasteur and Mendel to chemistry and genetics.

Bernays published the first book on public relations—*Crystallizing Public Opinion*—in the 1920s and taught the first college-level course on the subject. In 1947, Boston University offered the first degree in the field.

While PR may have seemed a good idea when Bernays first created it (though it was immediately used for causes that most today would agree were reprehensible), and although the PR field is filled with talented and effervescent people, it is important for writers and journalists to remember that, in journalism, PR can be a pejorative.

Alas, many less-than-ambitious journalists view PR as a resource that makes their job easier, like using *CliffsNotes,* instead of doing real reporting and writing. Thus, the real blame for the rise of PR is the indifference of reporters, writers, editors, and readers who have accepted manipulation and deception as a way of life.

Accordingly, a million customers bought Hillary Clinton's *Living History*—written by three ghostwriters and marketed with softball interviews with Ms. Clinton on the usual infotainment talk shows—because the distinction between PR and press was altogether blurred.

Ghostwriting is a special form of public relations. James Boswell, who followed Dr. Samuel Johnson around shamelessly, was probably the original "as told to" writer (unless you prefer the Apostle Paul). In 1791, Boswell produced *The Life of Samuel Johnson*, a work that is probably more widely read today than any of the writings of Johnson himself.

The "as told to" book or biography is, for obvious reasons, intended by the "author" (the subject of the book) to make her or him look as good as possible. While writers (interviewers) hired to "write" such books may draw a bit from historical facts, documents, or memos, in practice the core of the book is the "face to face" encounters with the subject. And the final interpretation, perspective, and color are imposed from on high, by either the subject directly or through PR advisers.

Ghostwriters nowadays are hired to check their trust at the door, and to reinvent someone who is well known. While the subject reflects on career and critics, the tape recorder drones on. Interviewing is nearly a stenographic function—taking notes on a version of events, not reporting on the events themselves. "As told to" authors often become "as lied to" writers, saying what the boss wants to say. The writer, often a journalist, has now become a part of the PR process.

William Novak, for example, regularly spins bestsellers out of other people's stories. "When I write material for people like Iacocca and Tip O'Neill, both common sense and simple ethics require that I show these remarks to my clients, who then decide if my sentences are true to their own language and sentiments," says Novak. "He is the golden mouthpiece of the nation's celebrities, a literary John Alden who can consistently woo—and win—the public in their behalf," reported *Time* magazine. In sum, such books are little different from massive PR jobs, with the involvement of a seemingly objective reporter who, it should be realized, is closely tied to the good graces, and PR efforts, of the subject.

PR types know the one inescapable truth that is part and parcel of the writing business: to write is to judge.

PR staffers are usually trained journalists, and they know how editors and writers think. With the job crunch and a graduate glut, many journalism majors who once dreamed of doing investigative work that would rival the achievements of Woodward and Bernstein are taking positions on the other side of the fence.

They are employed in what used to be called PR and what is now called the "department of communications" in companies, organizations, and the government. PR staffs bombard publications and newsrooms with phone calls and press packets suggesting stories on anything from a photo layout to a profile of a client with an ego for flattering news.

What are their goals? Well, the statement of purpose for one PR newsletter is "To provide subscribers with communication ideas and techniques they can put into action to persuade clients, influence peers and motivate employees; to help them earn approval, command respect, spur productivity, gain recognition and win public support."

Corporation PR departments are charged with creating and maintaining "the company image," which means attempting to manipulate and control the media in order to keep things "on message." This is surprisingly easy to do in the age of Handout Journalism, or via a PowerPoint presentation to tell the story. An interview, therefore, becomes a device to get the message out and establish uniformity in thinking and in selling the image.

Executives are often trained to meet the press, especially before a product launch. Each message is developed using "proof points" that are memorized for the occasion. One New York PR firm even offers a do-it-yourself training kit with six videotapes for anxious executives who want to learn how to "beat the press"—in 210 minutes of viewing time.

"Most media training sessions, private or group, work on the problem of executive nervousness, providing guidance on ways to relax before an audience or camera," says Peter Hannaford. Executives are told not to challenge a reporter, not to go off record, not to name competitors. "Some training programs," he adds, "will include 'ambush' interviews of one or more members of the group as they break for lunch."

PRs are journalism savvy. They know to check out directories and online resources to learn in advance "what this reporter is like." They are oh, so understanding; they feel your deadline pain and budget pressure.

Author and television commentator Jeff Greenfield captured the PR point-of-view when he called the media "a dangerous but potentially valuable animal. You must house it, feed it, pet it once in a while. You must never show it fear, or it will turn on you. You must gently, but firmly, guide it in the way you want it to go."

Working with the PR office

Sometimes a publicist can be an effective referee. Peggy Siegal often chaperones her clients through interviews to ensure that things run smoothly. Because a good publicist is persistent and often has great camaraderie with clients, this can occasionally work to a writer's advantage, especially if the celebrity is cantankerous or professionally inconsiderate.

When Patty Hearst tried to cancel interviews with the *New York Times* and the *Los Angeles Times* due to child-care problems in the eleventh hour, Siegal interceded: "We have commitments," she said sternly. Within hours Hearst had found a babysitter and was en route to the interviews. On another occasion, when actress Melanie Griffith was acting so ornery that the interviewer got up to call his editor and kill the story, Siegal interceded and made the actress behave and the reporter return to the table.

When you get assistance from a PR source, but the story has a negative impact on that office, you should consider giving a small warning in advance if you want that source to remain friendly. It allows the source to exercise a certain amount of damage control. One trait that Larry Speakes liked about *Washington Post* reporter David Hoffman was that he would call Speakes late in the afternoon and say, "We've got this. I just want you to know you're going to get hit with it when the paper hits the street at ten, so you can get a head start on it."

PRs don't like to be burned, of course. They make lists of who's been naughty and who's been nice to them in the media. They not only get angry; they get even. Publicist Peggy Siegal banned writer Lynn Hirschberg and columnist Susan Mulcahy from movie screenings and opening parties because they wrote pieces deemed critical of Siegal clients.

Other press officers have been known to play papers against each other, and punish reporters for critical stories by stalling or even denying interviews when possible. Media manager Raymond Dooley frustrated *Boston Globe* reporter Steven Marantz, who had written several stories critical of city hall, by refusing to talk to him for a profile Marantz was doing on Dooley. The *Globe* sent another reporter to interview Dooley for the profile— armed with Marantz's questions—and the answers were inserted in the final story, which carried Marantz's byline.

The ultimate taboo in working with PRs is to let the sources read the finished story before publication. This removes the reporter's control over his material and robs him of inherent journalistic responsibility. If you find yourself yielding on this point, you are now part of the PR process.

If a source wants to see the story, or the quotes used from an interview, you must say no. Otherwise, you are surrendering the only thing that reporting is all about: the final word. It's best if your publication prohibits any kind of preview by inquiring sources or their PR representatives. You can easily say, "Nothing personal—it's just policy."

Be fair, but be firm. The PRs might even respect you for your open, if tough style. "You have to remember one thing when dealing with the media," said one Hearst publishing executive, cautioning potential interviewees on the hard-nosed quality of some journalists. "You're never bigger than they are."

Working around the PR office

Some upper-level executives will hide behind the company PR department, which screens interview requests. If you find yourself stalled as PR staffers intrude in order to justify their jobs, don't try to go around the PR wall— go over it. With corporate PR people, there is an inevitable amount of red tape.

"Some of the best PR people I've worked with are in-house," says Jeffrey Seglin, a veteran business writer and author of *Selling Ice Cubes to Eskimos: America's New Breed of Entrepreneurs.* "So are some of the worst. If I get no help at all and he or she continues to insist I have to go through him, I'll put in a call directly to the CEO. As often as not, he'll talk to me."

PRs who screen calls have varying degrees of authority. Sometimes your requests will never make it to the subjects you want to speak with. "This doesn't happen as much with small businesses as it does with larger corporations or financial services corporations," adds Seglin. "The basic problem is often in the assumption that the best way to reach a source is through his PR person. That isn't always the case."

Seglin was working on a personal finance piece for a city magazine, and he wanted to get celebrities to comment on how they invested their money. "I had a hit list of people all over the board—TV personalities, actors, politicians, sports figures. At first I started to call the PR offices for the companies or agencies these people were involved with, and it began to consume enormous amounts of time. After the first few calls—and responses like, 'I'll have to get back to you on that'—I started to call my hit list directly. Very few turned me down."

Betsy Raskin, an editor at *Institutions* magazine, recalls how her publication tried for years to get an interview with Ray Kroc, the founder of McDonald's. "Because our magazine deals with the fast food industry, of course we wanted to speak with a leader and innovator like Kroc. But McDonald's has an incredible public relations network and they kept telling us that Kroc absolutely refused interviews."

When one of Raskin's colleagues spotted Kroc at the Whitehall Club in Chicago, however, she walked up to him slowly and introduced herself, saying, half-kiddingly, that *Institutions* was mad at him for refusing an interview.

"The hell I did," he said.

The interview that followed turned into a 16-page story for the magazine. "It also proved to all of us on the magazine that the best place to start is at the top, not with public relations people."

Common PR tactics

Here, then, drawn mostly from PR sources themselves, are some tricks of the PR trade to watch out for during interviews.

The "bridge" reply

The speaker offers a short answer to the immediate question that was asked, then moves on quickly to some larger theme that the individual or company wants to put across:

> Say: "Yes, that's important . . . but we also think . . ."

According to Jim Foy, editorial director at KNBC-TV in Los Angeles, this technique might as well be called what it really is: "Taking off into the wild blue yonder on another subject."

The "misunderstood" question

> Tell the interviewer anything you want; get your message
> across no matter what the question is. If caught at this, just say,
> "Oh, I must have misunderstood your question."

"Sorry, classified information"

> Say no. Refuse to answer a question—but offer a reason
> (privacy, security, budget secrecy).

"Wow, that's a tough one"

> Anticipate tough questions—what will they be?—and answer
> them as though you are surprised at the toughness.

The last word

> Always recap and get back to your message at the end of the
> interview. Have the final word and make sure it's "on message."

How to neutralize or overcome PR tactics

1. Establish your goals in advance.
Prep your subject and establish an agenda for the interview. Make it clear that you want to talk about his or her personal experiences, not the company line.

2. Bring them down from the sky.
During the interview, get him or her off-message by asking *how* questions:

> How do they do their job?
> How does a process work?
> How has a job changed over the years?

"Bring them down to reality," says a PR insider (not for attribution). "Most corporate messages are high in the sky."

3. Always cast questions to emphasize the positive.
If a company has had problems, for example, don't use the word *problem*. "When our clients hear questions about problems, they think the story is going to be about the problem," says Deep Promo, off record.

> *No:* What were the problems when you merged with Ajax?
> *Yes:* What did you learn from your last merger?

4. Finally, always check back when writing the story.
A follow-up interview is an opportunity to cut through the flackspeak that you may have to tolerate first time around. Call back. You might suggest:

> I'm afraid you are going to come off like someone who
> is hiding information.

This usually gets you to round two—and closer to reality. "We consider the interview and every question an opportunity to get our message across," says Deep Promo. "However, we don't want to come across as being overly promotional or having a separate agenda."

When in doubt about anything, check back with the source.

Then dig deeper.

CHAPTER 18

To Q&A or Not To Q&A?

THAT IS THE Q

The Q&A-style interview is a much maligned and misunderstood form. Some onlookers think it's easy to do, so why bother doing it at all? "You just put a microphone in front of the subject, throw out a few questions, transcribe the tape, and print the results." Right?

Wrong. A good Q&A will likely require as much work in the research and the writing as a narrative piece based upon interviews. It may even be more grueling to do—and more thankless in the end because so little of the work is evident to the reader.

When to abandon the Q&A

Yes, there are times when the Q&A is a clumsy, tiresome format. If a subject proves boring and colorless in responding to questions, that drabness is heightened by the Q&A approach. Likewise, someone who gives terse replies will seem abrupt in a Q&A. If replies are shorter than the questions, it looks as if the interview has not claimed the full attention of the subject.

When either of these journalistic turns occur—if your subject is lifeless or terse, or the material seems uneven—by all means kill the Q&A. Salvage what quotes you can and draft the piece instead as a short narrative profile. Toss out all of the *Q*s and, instead, polish your best *A*s.

Then, just write a brief introduction on your subject's background, noting: "We talked with Ms. Hagedorn, the chairman of the company, in her office recently, and she provided us with the following insights and information." Then set up each quote with a subhead that categorizes the nature of the observation.

On widgets

I have always had a fondness in my heart for widgets. The first time I saw one was in 1968, when I was just starting out. . . .

On the four-day workweek

If we can meet our production goals and our shipping schedules for customers in four days instead of five, I see no reason why we can't look at this notion in earnest sometime in the next millennium.

On the other hand, don't give up on the Q&A format altogether. There are many times when it is the perfect tool to handle an editorial problem.

When to turn to the Q&A

- To clarify a topic that is confusing or controversial. It is particularly effective when there are strong camps of thought on the issue. Sit down with the chairman of the board, or the company expert, and air the topic out. Under these circumstances, the Q&A is a clear window the reader can look through—without wondering too much what was involved in the questioning or editing process.

- If you have a subject who is live ammo in front of a microphone. Certain interviewees can take a question and run with it. They say things colorfully and know how to regale an audience with anecdotes, witty observations, and candor. This ideal subject is highly knowledgeable, but is also able to relate to readers new to the field.

  It helps if this subject appears to be having a good time on the job and in life at large—and if he or she seems to be enjoying the Q&A format.

- To draw together a variety of opinions on a multi-dimensional topic. In creating the questions, the writer can second-guess the questions a typical reader would have. The Q&A poses those questions for the readers, and then provides answers.

    When the racehorse Swale suddenly collapsed and died a few weeks after winning the Kentucky Derby, writer Steven Crist of the *New York Times* spoke with many experts on thoroughbred racing, horses, and veterinary medicine. Afterward, he drew up a list of questions that were in the average reader's mind. Then Crist asked these questions of himself. The Q&A, it turned out, was the ideal format for delivering such information, making readers feel represented at the finish line.

- As a sidebar to a longer piece on a complex topic. If your main article is on widgets as money-saving devices today, you can talk to the inventor of the widget and ask him a few questions about that first one and how it came to be. Formatted as a Q&A, it would make a bright sidebar feature, offering some background information and color for readers, and a nice visual breakup on a page of gray type, too.

If you have doubts about how effective your subject might be when faced with a microphone, prepare your discussion topics and give her a copy in advance. (Don't phrase them as questions, however, at this point, just as items you want to discuss.)

"I will probably have some other questions, Ms. Hagedorn, but these are the key topics our readers are interested in" might be a good approach. This allows the subject to think about matters in advance, and it should loosen up her answers considerably.

Often maligned, often abused, the Q&A remains a valuable tool for interviewers and for editors. It should not be tossed aside without serious examination.

For handling some editorial *Q*s, it may be the perfect *A*.

CHAPTER 19

Telephone Tactics

Phone interviews give you quicker, easier access to sources, no matter where they are. Neither wind nor rain nor small-town hideouts can keep an intrepid reporter from his sources. You can go across time zones and continents in a matter of moments. When a man suspected of being the notorious Unabomber was arrested in remote Lincoln, Montana, a Salt Lake City stringer for *People* magazine named Cathy Free got on the phone and called everyone in town to help piece together a portrait of the mysterious Ted Kaczynski.

Fortunately, the Lincoln directory (faxed to her by a school secretary) was only four pages long. Free's interviews gave context to the story, which chief of correspondents Joe Treen said "was way ahead of what the other magazines and newspapers had."

For Laura Hillenbrand, the phone was a way to beat the odds and come up a winner. Hillenbrand, author of *Seabiscuit*, the best-selling book about a horse that didn't know how to quit, battled chronic fatigue syndrome for sixteen years.

She was so debilitated that at times she wrote lying on her back with her eyes closed, scribbling on a pad held up at arm's length. Traveling to do interviews was impossible. Despite the handicap, she spoke with more than one hundred people for the book—all by phone.

Pros & cons

The biggest disadvantage when doing phone interviews, in most cases, is loss of visual clues that tell you how the interview is going. Some experts maintain that the visual, the nonverbal, accounts for up to 55 percent of communication. You cannot see the subject's eyes flicker with discomfort or light up with enthusiasm in response to a question. Rather, you are working like a blind person, without the special skills that a blind person develops to overcome the disadvantage.

On the other hand, some feel that the phone is far more effective as a communications device than face-to-face exchanges. "For many women, the phone is an instrument of intimacy," says Helen Berman, who leads seminars on the techniques of selling advertising by telephone. "Getting a phone in your room when you are a teenager is a big part of growing up for most females, and a phone conversation is a more intimate form of communication. It's a kind of intimacy that some men have to learn."

Depending on your skills in using the phone well and the comfort level of your interviewee in talking freely and expressively with someone who is not present in the room, your results will vary. However, in many cases, a phone interview is an excellent way to get the story quickly and with far less expense. According to a telemarketing manager, an average telephone sales call costs $15 compared to $230 for an average business-to-business field call, a ratio roughly applicable to journalistic interviews as well.

Besides the savings in cost, plus avoiding wear and tear on an interviewer on the road, another advantage of phone interviewing is the number of interviews you can do in a day. While a reporter in the field may be able to do two or three daily interviews—or perhaps four or five if working a district on a city beat—it is possible in that same time to make twenty phone calls and do up to seven or eight phone interviews without leaving the comforts of an office or home.

Phone interviews can also extend your work day by three hours— working from the West Coast, you can call Boston at 6 A.M. California time and catch people at the start of business. Or if you are in Boston, you can work into the early evening making your West Coast calls for interviews. Reporters for the *Los Angeles Times* who work in the Washington bureau put in a longer day than their peers, with the additional three hours of interviewing time they gain with their Pacific-time deadlines. The extra effort frequently leads to scoops and journalistic upsets.

Moreover, you don't always have to look your best. You can even make your calls from home, from your car, from the beach. Who's to know?

"Speaking as a hard-core phoneaholic, the only thing worse than having to look at the person I'm talking with is to have them looking at me," says syndicated columnist Michael Schrage. "I want the visual anonymity that telephones confer. I don't want a conversation where appearances matter."

This sort of invisibility can give a shy interviewer a kind of confidence not available when doing field interviews. Another advantage is that you can have materials to help you do the job better spread out all around your desk when you make the call: reference works, statistics, notes from other interviews.

"You can sound like a genius on the phone because you can look something up while the subject is starting to head in a direction that calls for some hard statistics. You can't do that in person," says Helen Berman.

Quickness & convenience

For the busy interviewee, the phone is also a time-saver. A phone interview may require only ten minutes, whereas a face-to-face encounter is likely to be an hour, which can prove a real turnoff for the subject with little time to spare.

Of course, the phone can also lead to the fast turndown. Some subjects will find it easier to say no on the phone. There is a famous *New Yorker* cartoon by Robert Mankoff that features a businessman on the phone, looking at his datebook, resisting an appointment. "No, Thursday's out," he says to his persistent caller. "How about never—is never good for you?"

"I guess it tapped into some real underlying truth," says Mankoff. "We all have busy, hectic lives filled with people we don't want to see, and who don't want to see us."

In interviewing, we often have to make do with the sources that will see us. In another cartoon—"Shoe," by Jeff MacNelly—a puzzled subject inquires, "Why did you choose me to interview for this project?"

The response: "Because you're the most prominent journalist in the state . . . who would return my phone call."

Making the connection

In some cultures, phone interviews are taboo. The Japanese, for instance, prefer not to do business of any sort over the phone. "A journalist must meet a source sometimes two or three times over tea before taking out a notebook," said Scott Shifrel in the *Washington Journalism Review*.

In other cases, when you call an expert at an institution that is hundreds or thousands of miles away, you may end up talking to a very flattered subject—if you are fortunate. Science writer Richard Rhodes ran into resistance from an eminent cosmologist, Allen Sandage, while completing an assignment for *Playboy* on developments in astronomy. Calling journalists "a pack of fools," the scientist told Rhodes that he wouldn't talk to him at all.

Rhodes was taken aback. For his story to have credibility, Rhodes needed the scientist, who had studied with the legendary Edwin Hubble, a pioneer in the measurement of the universe. "I don't normally bulldoze," said Rhodes. "I sit back and listen more than I push forward and demand. But I couldn't understand why a scientist wouldn't want to talk, however briefly, about his former teacher and his life's work."

The writer waited until evening, then called him again, this time at his Pasadena home. "I was persuasive. I'd done my homework. I could specify Sandage's field and work and rank—which is among the very highest of living astronomers. He was flattered." And Rhodes succeeded in getting the interview.

Timing

It helps to find out if your subject is a morning or afternoon person or a night owl. Ask your subject or the intermediary when you are setting up the interview, and then bend your phone calls accordingly.

Early morning interviews are often revealing ones. The early interviewer often gets the good quote. Employers often schedule interviews for early Monday, for example, "so you can detect any sign of weekend substance abuse," says Clayton Sherman in the hiring manual, *From Losers to Winners*.

Certainly, the difference between catching someone at a "good" or "bad" time can make the difference between a highly productive session and a frustrating confrontation. "Alertness, attention span and concentration can all be affected by an individual's personal peak time," says David Dinges, a biological psychologist at the University of Pennsylvania.

Don't be in too much of a rush. A subject may be turned off by a rushed, last-minute request for a "quick interview." When Margo Magee of *Buzz* magazine made several attempts to speak to Carol Stogsdill of the *Los Angeles Times*, Stogsdill complained that Magee had waited until the last minute to phone her. "I am not interested in 'adding a quote' to a story that is scheduled to go to press in a couple of hours," she said.

This is a curious posture from the senior editor of a daily newspaper whose reporters routinely ask subjects to do just that. Still, in general you will have more success when your potential interviewee feels there is a reasonable time to respond—and that he or she is being accorded a greater role in developing the story, rather than being pulled in at the end.

Getting through with your interview request

When you reach an office or company that uses voice mail, don't leave a message that is cryptic. "This is Joe Blow of the *Bugle*. Can you give me a call at 555-1234?" is not as enticing as:

> This is Joe Blow of the *Bugle*, and we are doing a story on Australian widgets. I understand that you are one of the world's leading expert on marketing widgets, and I'd like to spend some time with you—even if it's only ten minutes by phone.
> You can call me at 555-1234 during office hours, or if you want to reach me after hours or on the weekend, my cell phone is 123-5555. Thank you.

In short, leave a message that at least implies there is some benefit to be gained by talking with you. And leave enough details—a positioning state-ment—so that the subject knows who you are, what you are working on, and how he fits into your project.

When leaving a message, always give your phone number at the beginning of the call (for ease of access on playback), then repeat your phone number at the end. Also, with cell phones being somewhat crackly in nature, a single mention might not be recorded loud and clear.

No matter how enticing your message, don't expect a subject to return your call. Follow up. Be persistent and professional (but not pesty). Two or three calls with messages may be necessary to create the proper amount of guilt that will motivate a subject to call you back.

Remember, your goal at this point is simply to get a yes or no: "Will you do the interview?" You hope for a yes. If is it not feasible, you can accept a no. But evasion? Hardly.

Keep a record

Keep a record of attempts to reach a source so that you can offset any claims that you didn't call. The subject may hope to cast doubt on your reporting methods and raise questions of credibility. It happens.

Author Sally Bedell Smith tried to reach Sarah Ferguson, her majesty and Weight Watchers spokesperson, while writing *Diana in Search of Herself.* Smith had learned from other sources that Diana had stopped talking to Fergie a year before her death because Ms. Ferguson had claimed that she had contracted warts after borrowing a pair of Diana's shoes.

When Smith's book was published, Ms. Ferguson told journalists that the author had never called her for comment, adding, "I resent this woman who did not bother to ring me and personally speak with me before publishing her rubbish."

Smith's copies of letters she had sent to Fergie, and a call log noting that Ms. Ferguson's office had forwarded a message to the writer that an interview "was not something she wishes to do," defused the little contretemps. Interestingly, Fergie never refuted Smith's reporting, which was solid, warts and all.

Start as high as possible

If you have to go through a switchboard or a screening process, your goal is to go as high as you can up the company ladder. You want to avoid wasting time interacting with lower-rung people who may not be voices of authority. Moreover, underlings don't like end runs and are defensive about such maneuvers; rarely will you be referred upward in a company.

Therefore, you want to start as high as you can. If you are uncertain just who's who at Widget International, make an initial call to ask the switchboard, "Who handles your international widgets?" Then, once you've identified Mr. Big, call a little later and ask for him specifically.

"Will he know what this is about?" is the standard screen.

Tell the receptionist who you are, what you want—and what is in it for Mr. Big.

"You will find, too, that people at the top are easier to deal with," says Helen Berman. "They have more polished people skills, whereas those on the way up have only positional power. Their people skills are often rough, even primitive."

There are at least fifty ways to turn down an interviewer on the phone. "I'm not the one you want to talk to" is one brush-off. But don't be put off so easily. Transfers usually occur downward; it's more socially acceptable in companies.

If you are transferred, try to find an ally. Allies know shortcuts and strategies that can help you get through. Remember, there are two kinds of power in the workaday world: positional and personal. As an interviewer you may not have any positional advantage, but you can develop personal power as the conversation moves along.

Use purposeful ambiguity. When you are passed along to someone, say "I'm Joe Hagedorn from *X Magazine*, and Mr. Snuffler suggested that we talk."

If asked for supporting credentials, fax or e-mail them on the spot.

Celebrity interviews by phone

Doing celebrity interviews by phone can be tricky business. *Maui Scene* columnist Rick Chatenever says his worst experience was a phone interview with actor Robert Blake, set up by a studio to promote an upcoming movie about mobbed-up teamster boss Jimmy Hoffa.

"The interview had been set up by a publicist for the production," said Chatenever. "She was good at her job because she understood how things worked. She knew that celebrity journalism is a lot like real journalism, with one big difference: real journalism is designed to get at the truth. Celebrity journalism is designed not to. It's designed to inflate the illusion."

Chatenever knew the drill. He had read the press kit, converting it into remedial questions: "So, what kind of man was Jimmy Hoffa?"

Chatenever was ready for the customary answers—"He was a more complicated man than people realize"—but instead he ran into the testy side of a guy who really did not want to be on the phone. "Like, why was I asking him all these questions about Jimmy Hoffa? Who cared? . . . Oh, the TV movie? Who—the blank—cared about the movie?"

Sometimes, when you are speaking to a subject by phone, others are on the line or in the room. This can be a distraction, or you might be able to include the outsiders in the give and take. *Time* magazine's Frank Gibney was interviewing tennis pro John McEnroe on the phone about his autobiography, *You Cannot Be Serious*, which chronicles his marital and anger-management problems. In the background, Gibney could hear McEnroe's wife, Patty Smyth. "Since she's there with you, could Patty give you a grade for your development?" Gibney asked.

The result is an intimate glimpse of the give and take within a marriage. "Patty, would you like to give me a grade on my development over the past four years?" said McEnroe to his wife. "Yeah, like a school grade."

There was a pause on the line.

"A, B-plus or an A-minus, she says," reported McEnroe. "I don't know where that means I started . . . What? She said I started at D. I was a good dad, but I guess that was the only thing that kept me from failing."

Newsday gossip columnist Susan Mulcahy, who had done stories on the making of the movie *Bright Lights, Big City*, had spoken several times with publicist Peggy Siegal. Still, she called Siegal once more, reaching her at a cabana at the Beverly Hills Hotel, to confirm a rumor that Phoebe Cates and Keifer Sutherland had been signed up to be in it.

Siegal, furious, began to jump up and down, spitting angry. She wanted to give that scoop to another publication. "You are obsessed with this story!" she shouted into the phone. "Leave it alone!"

What Siegal didn't know was that Mulcahy was phoning her from a lounge chair near the cabana, watching her squirm. As they say in the land of the LaLa, it was quite a scene. The interviewer always rings twice.

CHAPTER 20

More Tips for Successful Phone Interviews

Win, lose, or draw, the majority of interviews for publication today are conducted by phone. Here is advice for getting the most out of your own phone sessions.

1. Clear the line and clear the deck.

If you are sharing a line with others in the office, tell them you are doing an interview. No interruptions. Turn off call waiting (*70), which will be reinstated when you hang up. Never keep anyone on hold for more than thirty seconds.

Know your energy levels for phone work. A day of interviewing should be approached more like a marathon than a sprint. Work on the phone during your high periods; do backup work during middle periods; and take a break or eat lunch when your energy level is low.

At home, try to avoid answering the phone when you are in the kitchen or otherwise engaged. Writer Jennifer Mendelsohn explained the dilemma of being caught during lunch in her Washington, D.C., home office:

> Me, mouth full of tuna: "Mmmmmmllo?"
>
> Very important person I really need to talk to: "Yes, I'm returning your phone call about [very important story I'm working on]."
>
> What to do? I've let pizzas burn to a crisp because I was too embarrassed to interrupt a conversation to turn off the

oven—"Ambassador, can you just bear with me a second while I tend to my Lean Cuisine?" simply isn't the kind of question that elicits professional respect.

Once, unable to confess to a caller that he had caught her mid-lunch, Mendelsohn scrawled all the notes from an interview in the margins of an old newspaper.

2. Prepare to keep the conversation moving forward.

If you need to do three interviews for a story, you should have an array of nine or ten prospects in your initial round of calls. We know from tele-marketers that people are away from their phones at a 3:1 ratio.

We know, too, that once you get a subject on the line, the conversation is much faster-paced than an in-person chat. Forget small talk. Let's get on with the business here.

On the phone, you must talk faster and cover more ground than you would in person; yet you must also go in small steps. It's best to work in a structured but not script-like manner. Have a list of topics you want to cover, tell the subject what the topics are at the outset, and then hang in for a fast conversational ride.

Your opening should be confident. You should sound relaxed, yet interested. Confirm with the subject that it is convenient for him to talk.

Ask "Do you have a few minutes?" if it is an unscheduled interview.

"Is this indeed a good time to talk as we planned?" is most courteous if the time has been set in advance.

3. Be prepared for the instant interview.

Occasionally, when you phone to set up an interview, the subject will say something like, "I'm leaving for three weeks in the Yukon tomorrow. Can we do this now?"

Your response, of course, is: "Absolutely." Be prepared for an instant interview.

"Um, no, I'd rather call you back on Thursday" can sound rather limp and unenthusiastic. (Get his Yukon phone number for follow-up, however.)

4. Advise your subject that you are recording.

If the subject doesn't want to be recorded, you can often overcome resistance by pointing out that it is in her or his best interest: "I'm recording our conversation so that I can listen to it again and be one-hundred percent accurate."

Other good reasons to offer: "By recording our conversation, I won't have to slow you down with my taking notes." Or, "No one else is going to hear this tape. I can make you a copy for your files as well, if you wish."

Caution: secret tape recordings are not only unethical in the writing trade, they can also be hazardous to your publishing health. In most states, laws prohibit the tapping of a telephone line without the consent of all parties using the phone.

Freelance journalist Eric Ford intercepted a cell-phone call between actor Tom Cruise and his then-wife Nicole Kidman. Ford sold the tape to a tabloid, which printed parts of the conversation as a marital spat. When the actor's representatives alerted authorities, Ford ended up in court pleading guilty to federal wiretapping charges. He was fined and sentenced to six months in a halfway house and three years' probation.

5. Agree on the length of the interview.

Subjects do not usually like lengthy open-ended conversations on the phone. Establish up front how long you will require—twenty minutes, half an hour, whatever—and put the subject at ease with your timetable. Then stick to it.

"Our half hour is nearly up," you might say as time winds down, even if you haven't been able to cover all topics. If you need more time with a subject who has to go, try to get a commitment before the call is over. "When is a good time for us to talk again?" is one way to get on a subject's busy schedule.

If the conversation is going well and time is not a consideration, talk on—but only after you have acknowledged your original understanding. This also binds you and the subject, helping to build rapport.

Be ready for the quick hang-up if the conversation falters. Fred Goodman once tried to interview skittish talent manager Sandy Galin, who finally consented to a telephone interview from a car. Suddenly,

Galin said, "I'm going into my parking lot now—we're going to get cut off," signaling that the interview was over. Thereafter he was not interested in scheduling any more calls. "Use your imagination," he said, hanging up the phone.

6. Take notes, including a tape index.
Using a headset (Klantronic is a popular brand of choice among telemarketers) will protect you from neck stress. You'll sound much better, believe me. It also frees your hands to take great notes on the keyboard.

When taking notes, be sure to take notes on what *you* say as well. Good notes should be dialogues.

Also, as the interview progresses, create an index of topics for each side of each cassette—keyed to the tabulator on your recorder:

> 125—discussion of decision to sell the company
>
> 210—story of meeting spouse
>
> 355—budget plans for next decade

This will enable you to return to key tales and topics you want to locate on a tape, without having to go through the whole interview on a hunt-and-search mission.

7. Don't leave your own interview.
Give complete attention to the call, and do not allow interruptions. On the phone, it's easy to do other things while the subject talks on (and on). Avoid the temptation to give in to visual distractions.

Instead, close your eyes.

Why? Because it enables you to concentrate. It prevents you from doing other things like writing letters, reading the newspaper, scanning your electronic mail, nibbling a fingernail. Closing your eyes allows you to give your undivided attention to the task of listening.

8. A little etiquette goes a long way.

- Use the subject's name occasionally, but not repeatedly.

- Limit your own talking to questions and follow-up.

- Don't interrupt. Use positive interjections.

9. Consider the conference call.

Bringing two or more sources together for an interview can create a lively crossfire. Joseph Kahn of the *Boston Globe*, for instance, used a conference call to interview author Stephen King and Red Sox relief pitcher Tom Gordon, as King's bestselling novel *The Girl Who Loved Tom Gordon* climbed the charts. The give-and-take was lively; the quotes congenial.

When you go beyond two subjects, of course, the risk of vocal overlap goes up dramatically. Teleconference consultant Charlotte Purvis recommends addressing questions to specific individuals, asking participants to identify themselves when they speak, and keeping a list of the participants in front of you so you don't forget people who haven't spoken in a while.

10. You've got to have a closer.

How do you end a phone interview? It's good manners to let the subject hang up first, after giving clear signals that the interview is completed. Usually, a simple "Well, it's been good talking with you. . . ." will get you off the phone and on to your next interview.

Occasionally, you will encounter the little old long-winded interviewee who is far too happy to talk, and talk, and talk. As a last resort, to conclude an interview, knock four times loudly on your desk.

"Mr. Hagedorn, someone's at my door" is your exit line. "I'll get back to you if I need any additional material."

11. Make notes of any follow-up needed immediately.

When you hang up, or as soon as possible, ask yourself what follow-up action is necessary. Flesh out your notes while they are still warm. Make a list of other calls to make as a result of this interview. You may even realize you want to schedule a follow-up call with the subject you have just spoken with for a second conversation or point of clarification.

Setting up a phone-interview center

Here is some advice on creating a comfortable, professional setup in your home for doing phone interviews.

1. Select a spot.

If you are doing phone interviews on a regular basis, make yourself comfortable. Design a cave, a nest, where you have everything on hand you need to conduct an interview—or to handle a callback at an unexpected time.

The work area should be quiet, and you should be able to control any interruptions.

If you don't want your subject to know you are calling from home, tapes of office background sounds are available. Based upon the premise that hearing is believing, a CD called *Office Chatter*, for instance, contains sixty minutes of ringing phones, clacking typewriters, sliding file drawers, and a female voice occasionally murmuring, "May I help you?" Anyone at the other end of the phone would think you are working in a busy, fully staffed office.

"It enhances your image over the phone," says *Office Chatter* producer Laura Newman. "It's no more deceptive than trying to look your best by wearing a suit to work."

2. Get the right equipment.

- A comfortable chair with good support.

- Access to a phone line.

- A tape hookup connected to the phone line allows you to record calls with greater clarity; other options are devices that are placed on the phone's earpiece or a separate free-standing microphone.

- A lightweight headset will keep your hands free to browse files or take notes on the keyboard. Some of you might prefer to use a portable phone (if you like to pace while you talk). But in most cases, you will find anything besides a headset tiring to hold in place over the course of a long interview, and hard to handle if you need to write notes.

- A work surface to write notes by hand—or to support your computer keyboard or laptop, which will allow you to take notes directly into an electronic file.

- Shelves or surfaces where research materials are immediately accessible. These materials might include statistical research, competitive data, and clips or notes from previous stories or interviews.

3. Get an answering machine or service.
An important piece of gear is a phone answering service, or, for most, an answering machine. You will need one to get interviews, making it easy for sources to get back to you with a message. Invest in a good one: one that takes messages longer than thirty seconds and that enables you to check your messages from remote locations.

Here are some tips for leaving messages:

- When you step away from your desk, leave a fresh message saying when you will return. Be as specific as possible, and don't use background mood music or cornball announcements; play it straight and professional.

- Good telephone manners are polite, if artificial. "Your call is very important to us" may be right up there with "Have a nice day" in encomiums that aren't quite sincere. Still, it's always nice to be nice.

- Don't leave a personal message or a family all-in-one message on the machine. Get a second phone line for your professional use, or at least set up a separate electronic mailbox to direct callers to the right message.

- If you are in an office that uses voice mail, the rules are the same. Someone calling in should know whether you are down the hall for two hours or out of town for two weeks.

4. Make sure others can find your number.

When you live by the phone interview, it is important that others be able to find your number without great difficulty. Certainly we are all entitled to a private sanctuary, but when your phone number is unlisted, you risk losing a story.

"You have to be accessible," said Bob Woodward of the *Washington Post*. Woodward is listed in the D.C. directory as Robert Woodward. "People always know they can reach me anytime." Likewise, Gay Talese is in the Manhattan white pages.

Journalist Allan Wolper recalls the time his wife picked up their phone and an operator announced, "You have a collect call from Willie Horton at the Maryland State Correctional Institution." She knew the caller was the killer-rapist who, as the unintentional star of a political TV commercial, helped wreck the presidential campaign of Michael Dukakis.

"Not the kind of person a woman—even a woman journalist—would give her home phone number to," said Wolper. "But a story is a story. She interviewed Horton about his life as a celebrity criminal and chastised me for giving our home number to one more murderer."

While Wolper and spouse disagree on how much privacy a journalist is entitled to, their phone number remains in the New York phone directory ten years after Willie Horton called. "There is a good reason for being there," adds Wolper.

"Leakers appreciate the fact that they can catch a reporter at home away from the Big Brother electronic spying devices proliferating in corporate America."

CHAPTER 21

The E-mail Interview

To E or not to E . . . that *used* to be the question. For many interviewers today, however, there is no question about it. E-mail is *the* answer for getting answers. "You've got mail" may mean a trip to the post office for some, but for interviewers, it means get online.

There is some resistance to what e-mail hath wrought, of course. Some traditional interviewers concede that e-mail is useful, but mostly as a great way to follow up with sources, asking them to verify information already gathered during face-to-face or phone interviews.

"Purists argue that e-mail is typed, not spoken, and lets sources invent their own quotations rather than participate in spontaneous exchanges with the writer," says author and Iowa State University journalism director Michael Bugeja. On the other hand, he notes, "Realists believe that e-mail is speech and more accurate. Better still, the writer has a transcript when a source denies that he or she said something."

An Instant Message interview has much of the give-and-take dynamic of a spoken exchange, for instance. And when you need a quick response, using e-mail is about the same as getting on the phone for an answer to a question or two.

Is an e-mail exchange a conversation, and therefore really an interview? Let's just call it an *enterview.*

E-mail exchanges for publication go back at least as far as the early 1990s, when Howard Rheingold, futuristic editor of the *Millennium Whole Earth Catalog*, discussed the once and future catalog with the editors of

U.S. News & World Report entirely by e-mail. Since then, e-mail has gradually replaced the fax machine to procure answers and information from elusive subjects.

During the messy divorce proceedings between Donald and Ivana Trump, for instance, the warring couple traded barbs through gossip columnist Liz Smith, whose fax machine was used to obtain the daily sordid details on a prenuptial agreement and lawyers doing verbal battle.

Likewise, after noticing that a French champagne producer was completing the purchase of hundreds of acres of Oregon farmland, a food-and-wine writer for the *Statesman Journal* in Salem, Oregon, sent a fax request for interviews with the winery's managers in France. He also was able to supplement his request with sample clips and credentials.

Today, many publications highlight e-mail as an interviewing device in their pages. *Fast Company* magazine columnist Anne Kreamer, for example, interacts with an e-mail guest each month, resulting in a Q&A with a business leader.

Meanwhile, *Entertainment Weekly* reported that "online interviews are becoming the new voice of Hollywood celebs." The reason? Control.

"The e-mail interview gives all the power to the interview subject since it leaves little or no room for follow-up or for pressing for answers to tough questions," says John Frank, bureau chief for *PRWeek*. In his opinion, the process is too one-sided and should be the tool of last resort, to be used only "with sources you absolutely have to get some comment from for a story."

Other drawbacks

Doing an enterview is not without other problems, of course. With high-profile subjects, you can never be certain whether the words you are reading on your screen are original utterances from the subject or pseudo-quotes run through (or created by) an intermediary—a publicist or PR assistant, perhaps—whose job is not merely to screen and control questions, but also to filter out the *mans*, *likes*, and *you knows*. The result can be a transformation of a fresh response into carefully worded answers that sound more like legal briefs than real conversation.

For the interviewer, this can mean a very dull exchange, or wading through responses that have been scripted for an audience the subject wants to reach—though the good news is that in cyberspace, no one can hear you scream.

Nor do enterviews work when you are doing a story that calls for color or scene setting, where you need to describe someone and capture the mood and attitude of a "day in the life" of a profile subject. No, that requires some hanging out and face-to-face time. Because so much insight is communicated visually, face-to-face interviewing is always best for such endeavors. Second best is the telephone.

Another drawback of the enterview is you won't get "off the record" information that is often The Good Stuff in a close encounter of the word kind. Enterviews are on the screen and on the record, and that's all, folks.

There are, of course, guerrilla tactics for getting around these inconveniences. But first, let's consider the many advantages of the enterview.

Advantages

1. Quick start.
You always know that your message will get through. Unlike the phone interview, you don't have to spend hours or days playing telephone tag to start the process.

2. Go anywhere.
The enterview transcends time zones and international boundaries. You can enterview sources all over the world—anywhere, any time—which is a strong advantage as the globalization of publishing continues.

3. Save money.
E-mail is one of the cheapest means to reach sources, and allows you to solicit them to send you their comments and opinions at little cost.

4. Flexibility.
You can enterview subjects from anywhere—using a cell phone or a laptop or a desktop computer. Nothing constricts you or pins you or your subject down to the confinements and limitations of a particular place.

Also, you don't have to worry about looking your best, and you can send your queries off anytime. You can start an enterview in your robe and slippers at two o'clock in the morning, then go to bed with the comfortable knowledge that your queries will be part of the recipient's morning mail.

5. Save time.

Enterviews are quick action. You can get answers to questions quickly, within the hour. The "getting to know you" conversation that often precedes an interview is eliminated. This is even faster than the phone interview, which can take hours or days to arrange and complete. For writers on deadline, the quick delivery of enterviews is key.

6. Round-ups made easy.

When you need a little bit of information from a lot of people, or an array of opinions on a single topic, the enterview is the perfect tool. Stories like "101 Money-Saving Ideas for Widget Manufacturers," for instance, can be developed quickly by sending an e-mail to an array of sources with a single query:

> What cost-saving ideas have you developed at your widget
> factory in the past year?

7. Instant Q&As.

For writers on assignment to do a short Q&A piece, the enterview is a natural. You e-mail the *Q*s. Your subject gets back to you with the *A*s.

8. Assist challenged sources.

For the subject who does not like to get into conversations, who likes to take some extra time to answer questions, or who may have a stammer or speech problem, the enterview is a godsend.

"I'm shy on the phone," author and editor Jenna Glatzer told *Writer's Digest*, "so I love doing interviews by e-mail."

Some sources have disabilities that make the enterview necessary. David Carr of the *New York Times*, for instance, faxed questions to Bob Guccione when the publisher was unable to speak publicly because of the effects of throat cancer. Guccione (or a spokesperson . . . you never know) faxed back his responses.

9. Protect sources.

Consider reporter Nicole Itano of the *Christian Science Monitor*, who couldn't do an in-person interview for a story about the government of Zimbabwe because the government had become quite hostile to foreign correspondents. Itano, based in South Africa, had been denied a visa to visit Zimbabwe. Many local journalists had been jailed. Moreover, Cathy Buckle, the woman Itano wanted to interview, was conducting an e-mail campaign against a harsh government and preferred not to speak on the phone, which was being monitored by government watchdogs.

"She didn't want to say something that might get her arrested," said the reporter. "By doing the interview online, she felt she could more carefully choose her words."

10. Wordsmith appeal.

Certain types of interviewees excel in the e-mail format. One is the person who writes more lucidly or poetically than he or she speaks. In such case, a written response, asked and delivered through the e-mail format, can provide well-turned phrases. While they may lack the spontaneity of a verbal conversation, it can make up for that in its literary quality, while still retaining some of the veneer of the conversation.

11. Eliminate chore work.

Nothing is more tedious for the interviewer than listening to a taped conversation and transcribing quotes. With the enterview, the responses you receive are already transcribed—an enormous saving of time and toil.

12. Eliminate lawsuits.

It's unlikely you will ever hear an enterview source say, "I was misquoted." The words are right there on the screen for all to see and agree on before you go to press with a quote.

How to conduct an e-interview

When handled with common sense and consideration of its special nature, the e-mail interview is a powerful weapon in your arsenal. Here are five key guidelines.

1. Approach with care.

If your source is hard to get for an enterview, point out the many advantages of the format to her or him. Questions can be answered at their convenience, and they can take their time (up to a point) to formulate their responses with care.

In addition, e-mail takes the least amount of time from a source's busy schedule. It is usually very specific about the type of information sought, not a rambling fishing expedition, which many sources hate.

The initial approach may be by phone, in order to obtain a source's cooperation (and to obtain the e-mail address, or to confirm an address you may have on hand). Paving the way by phone will give you a bigger and better response, as your e-mail is then expected and more likely to get through; large portions of cold e-mail messages are zapped as spam.

"People are becoming increasingly concerned about junk e-mail and privacy," says Mark O'Keefe, national correspondent, Newhouse News Service, "so be sure to identify yourself and the publication you're working for. Make it clear you're asking for e-mail answers that may be published."

2. Be organized.

As we know, you only get one chance to make a good first impression, and that is true online as well as in person. It's important that you look your best online, which means being organized and conveying that attitude to your source. It is usually best to send your message at night or first thing in the morning, so it is present in the inbox when the typical person checks his or her e-mail for the day.

Remember, this is an enterview, not an Instant Message chat. Be a little formal at the outset, using Mr. or Ms. in your greeting. Include your phone number (including cell phone) and a mailing address, along with pertinent information about yourself and the publication for which you are writing.

Give a deadline. Many people try to handle their e-mail on a timely basis, clearing the decks of inquiries by end of day. Chances are that you will receive a response within 24 hours, but just to make certain you have your answers next day, give a noon deadline and keep an eye on your e-mail inbox for action.

3. Be focused.

When you send questions in advance, the rule is brevity: no more than five questions for openers. Make certain your questions are clear and easy to understand at first reading. An ambiguous question may be subject to misinterpretation, or to the droll reply.

On the eve of a multimedia reunion known as "The Beatles Anthology," George Harrison agreed to be interviewed by *Newsweek* on the condition that the interview be conducted by fax. Harrison, known for his elusiveness and his wit, was asked, "When you see McCartney and/or Starr these days, do you hug or shake hands?"

He faxed back, "Yes."

The main reason any celebrity agrees to an e-mail exchange, of course, is to promote. Under these circumstances, the prudent enterviewer will keep a ready supply of safe queries on hand—such as, What are your cinematic influences?—"lest he or she end up presiding over dead space or an online encounter session," says Patricia Dilucchio, writing in *Entertainment Weekly*.

"Stars don't want to talk about their ex-wives, former boyfriends, or more successful siblings," she noted.

4. Go back and forth.

The good thing about the e-mail exchange is that it is conducive to a number of rounds. It's a different kind of conversation, but still can have some of the back-and-forth quality of conversation on screen. Net-savvy readers are quite accustomed to e-mail exchanges, with their short, blurby comments, and quick, off-the-cuff, quirky style.

Once you get a response, consider a follow-up question or two. You can select the portion of the subject's initial response that contained the most interesting information, and ask the person to elaborate on it a little.

However, when reporters for the *New York Times* tried to interview Republican presidential adviser Karl Rove for a story on his expanding role in the White House, they reported that "Mr. Rove declined to be interviewed for this article, writing in an e-mail message, 'I'm not deeply involved in foreign policy!' Asked to elaborate, he restated in a subsequent e-mail message, 'I am not deeply involved.'"

In this context, an e-mail exchange is not exactly an interview, but it is most certainly a response, an answer, a reply—and certainly preferable to "no comment" or stone silence.

5. Follow up by phone or face to face.

Always consider a follow-up by phone—if any responses to your questions are evasive, unclear, or if you just want to live happily ever after with an unambiguous reply. A phone follow-up might also offer a chance to pose a more complex or open-ended question to draw your subject out in an extended conversation.

To keep the dialogue going and broaden the topics, you might even want to consider asking your source to do a face-to-face follow-up interview.

Such is the lure of the e-mail encounter. It is generally simple, brief, and convenient—but it can be the start of something big.

CHAPTER 22

Best Questions

While it's often helpful to have some off-the-rack questions on hand, it's always best to use them to make a connection to the subject's real life. Using canned questions can be likened to walking on a beach with a metal detector. When you get a hit, start digging and forget everything else—including the next canned question.

For professionals on career tracks

What do you hope to accomplish in the next three years?
    Five years? Ten?
What's the dumbest decision you ever made?
What lesson(s) have you learned from a mistake
    or error in judgment?
How do you deal with pressure?
What's the biggest issue facing your field today?
Do you ever work as a mentor to young people in the
    business? What do you tell them? How do you coach
    them?
What advice would you give to someone starting out
    in this business?
What motivates you?
What is the biggest professional risk you've taken?
What did you learn in college or graduate school
    that helped you in your profession?
If you could retire and start a second career,
    what would you do?

What do you do to get away from work? Can you shut it off?

What is your proudest professional achievement?

Who has been a role model in your life?

How might a colleague describe your work habits?

At the end of a long day, what's your idea of a perfect evening?

To what personal traits do you attribute your success?

What traits do you admire in other people?

What professional challenges have you had to face?

As a youngster, what did you want to be when you grew up?

What adjectives might a colleague use to describe your
work habits?

What challenges have you faced on the job?

What historical figures do you most admire?

What personal sacrifices have you made to stay competitive?

What have you learned that you might not know if you
had not chosen this field?

Can you give me an example of an irritant you might
encounter in your work, something that annoys you, dis-
tracts you, that you wish you didn't have to put up with?

In a typical day, how much of your time is spent on
the phone, computer, in meetings, at your desk?

What inspires you?

What challenges you?

How would you describe yourself? What are your
character traits?

What do you enjoy about your work? Dislike?

How is it you have been able to be successful in
this competitive field?

How would you categorize your relationships with
peers in your field?

What constitutes a safety net for you? What makes
you feel safe?

What zaps your energy? What rejuvenates it?

What would you like us to know about you that
we haven't asked?

Did there come a time in your career where you were faced with a "fork in the road"? If so, do you ever revisit the decision you made or didn't make?

Work habits

Can you tell me about any project you had to tackle where you had to meet a hard deadline? What did you do?

Do you work best in the morning or evening?

How often do you fail at work?

For someone who has led a company to success

What role have you played in turning the company around?

What impact did you think you could have before taking your present position?

What would you be doing if you weren't in this business?

What inspired you to get into this business?

What's the most disappointing business trend that you've seen lately?

What's the smartest business decision you've made?

What advice would you give to someone starting out in the business?

What do you think you accomplished at the company?

Name one person you are dying to work with.

What's your biggest fear?

How do you turn around a big ship like this?

Is failure ever valuable?

Questions about a co-worker's job performance

Can you describe his work habits?

How reliable is he?

Does he meet deadlines consistently?

How much direction does he need?

Does he work well with others?

Is he self-motivated? Is he assertive?

What are his job strengths?

What areas does he need to work on?

Reading habits

What's the best book you've read in the last year?

What's your favorite quote?

Who is your favorite author?

Do you check the bestseller lists when buying a book?

Personal pleasures

What makes you happy?

When are you happiest?

Do you have a prized possession?

What country would you like to visit but haven't?

What three CDs would you want with you on a desert isle?

What part of the world would you like to visit but haven't yet?

Do you have a favorite band?

Do you ever memorize song lyrics?

If you could share a taxi from the airport with any celebrity—
who would you choose?

Anxieties

What's your biggest fear?

Beyond death, what do you think is the biggest fear
of most people?

What are your goals?

What are your aspirations?

What is your greatest wish?

Getting to the sensitive side

When you look in a mirror, what do you see?

If you could eliminate a trait of your own, what would it be?

Can you tell me the story of your growing-up years,
the first ten years of your life?

If you could go back and be a certain age again, what age
would it be?

Who influenced you more—your mother or your father?

What did your father do? Your mother?

Were you ever bullied in school?

Lifestyle influences

> How has California (or New York, Texas, etc.)
>   influenced your life?
> What's your favorite place in Los Angeles?
> Give me three words to describe yourself.
> What is your personal motto?
> What is your favorite quote?

Questions from *Vanity Fair*'s last-page "Proust Questionnaire"

(Proust was a brooding sort of fellow, one who like to explore life's deep questions of ultimates and whose characters were prone to intense bouts of self-examination.)

> What is your idea of perfect happiness?
> What is your greatest fear?
> Which historical figure do you most identify with?
> What is the trait you most deplore in yourself?
> What is the trait you most deplore in others?
> What is your favorite journey?
> What do you consider the most overrated virtue?
> On what occasion do you lie?
> What do you dislike most about your appearance?
> Which living person do you most despise?
> Which words or phrases do you most overuse?
> What is your greatest regret?
> Which talent would you most like to have?
> If you could change one thing about yourself,
>   what would it be?
> If you could change one thing about your family,
>   what would it be?
> What do you consider your greatest achievement?
> If you were to die and come back as a person or thing,
>   what do you think it would be?
> What is your most treasured possession?
> What do you regard as the lowest depth of misery?
> What is your most marked characteristic?

What talent would you most like to have?

What is the quality you most like in a man?

What is the quality you most like in a woman?

What do you most value in your friends?

Who are your favorite writers?

Who is your favorite hero of fiction?

Who are your heroes in real life?

If you could have dinner with three people, living or not, whom
would you choose and why?

How would you like to die?

What is your motto?

Oprah's big question (from the last page in *O* magazine)

What do you know for sure?

Variations on that old standby, "How Did You Feel . . . ?"

What were you thinking?

What went through your mind?

How did you decide that?

Let's go through your thinking process
when that happened . . .

Questions from last-page department, *Details* magazine

When was the last time you . . .

Lost all composure?

Were cruel to an animal?

Had impure thoughts?

Abused your power or celebrity?

Did something reckless?

Gave in to peer pressure?

Spoke another language?

Exposed yourself?

Probing the personality

Interviews for personality profiles are all about individuality—explaining why someone lives where he lives, behaves as she does, and so forth. Your questioning should accentuate the individualistic, and the answers should explain why this individual is not quite part of the crowd.

Can you name five things you like very much?

Five things you dislike?

Did you have a happy childhood?

Describe the incident in your childhood that you think
most affected you.

How do you feel about your mother? Your father?

What are your favorite hobbies?

How have your hobby interests changed over the years?

Do you pray? Do you meditate? Chant? Do yoga?

Do you consider yourself a religious person?

What are your politics?

What is your philosophy of life?

What is your attitude toward money?

If you had a million dollars, how would you spend it?

What is your idea of a perfect vacation?

How do you usually spend a workday?

Have you had any medical difficulties?

Have you had any experiences with death?

What kind of education did you have, and how do
you feel about it?

How do you think other people react to you?

What are you proudest of?

What are you most ashamed of?

How do you feel about food?

What do you dream about?

What makes you feel good?

What sort of work do you try to avoid or put off?

What person do you think has influenced you the most?

Are you athletic?

How methodical are you?

What are your chief taboos?

How much traveling have you done?

Can you describe a situation in which you feel you behaved
    courageously?

Do you see yourself as a self-centered person?

Do you see yourself as a loving person?

Do you see yourself as a popular person?

What is your definition of power?

What do you see as the responsibilities of power?

How artistic are you?

What are your plans for the future?

How idealistic are you?

How realistic are you?

How successful are you?

What are five things that you most often object to
    in other people?

Name three things that you most object to in yourself.

How gullible are you?

Do you believe that the end justifies the means?

What do you worry about most?

Do you know of anything worth dying for?

For you, what makes life worth living?

How do you react to the current world situation?

Which changes now taking place in the world should be
    encouraged, and which resisted?

What ideas now popular in our society do you consider
    potentially dangerous?

What mistakes in your life have you learned from?

Ultimately, how would you like to be remembered?

Barbara Walters' questions for celebrities

(Tears Not Always Optional.)

To actress Renée Zellweger:

> How did the role in *Chicago* change you as an actress?
>
> Let's go back to your childhood . . .
>
> What was the first movie you ever saw?
>
> What did your parents teach you? Your mother? Your father?

Zellweger mists at recollections of her mother; not quite tears. Barbara continues:

> Take me back seven years ago, before you got your big role in *Jerry Maguire*. What were you doing?
>
> Is anyone in your life now?
>
> Any sense of a biological time clock? Marriage? Children?
>
> And what's next?
>
> I've read that you need serenity. Tell me about that.

After asking Zellweger if she wants to find true love, Baba closes, saying: "I hope it happens. That's my wish for you."

To actress Julianne Moore:

> Why do you prefer to play these sad, difficult women?
>
> When you first met your [younger] husband, did the nine-year difference bother you?
>
> What has motherhood meant to you?

(The tears flow.)

> You have said, "If somebody said 'you can't be an actor any-more,' it might be a relief." What did you mean by that?

And in closing: "You've given people a lot of pleasure," says Baba. "I hope that gives you a lot of pleasure."

To actor Nicholas Cage:

> At what age did you really know you wanted to act?
>
> Your father was an eccentric. Tell me about him.
>
> Let's talk about your mother, a woman you love very much, but who was difficult . . . Did you ever worry that you might inherit your mother's illness? [schizophrenia]
>
> Everything I read about you describes you as weird, eccentric, wild. What three adjectives would you use to describe yourself?

Cage chooses shy, romantic, and emotional, saying the reports Barbara read were "part of a plan to create an image."

> Let's talk about something I read about and clear up myths. Are you obsessed with Elvis Presley?
>
> Do you think someday you will find the perfect mate?
>
> What's been the best time of your life?

"Right here, right now, with you," says Cage. Baba closes with: "Awwww."

Barbara Walters & the hypotheticals

Barbara Walters once revealed to the *New York Times* her five "foolproof" questions for the over-interviewed:

> 1. If you were recuperating in a hospital, who would you want in the bed next to you, excluding relatives?
> 2. What was your first job?
> 3. When was the last time you cried?
> 4. Who was the first person you ever loved?
> 5. What has given you the most pleasure in the last year?

Walters says that question three is "an especially good one for comedians. They're hard to interview because you're always the straight man."

When the *Times* asked Walters how *she* would answer her foolproof questions, she demurred, "Uh, well . . . I don't think I want to. It would take me too long to think of some good answers." (Which may confirm that the most difficult interviewees are often interviewers.)

Walters' first foolproof question, and many similar icebreaker questions, are hypothetical. And the interviewer skates at his own risk.

Walters recalls the time she asked Prince Philip of Great Britain if, in the event England elected a president, he would have enjoyed being a politician. Philip replied, without warmth, that this was a hypothetical question, which he normally didn't answer.

"I was crushed," says Walters, "but I learned a valuable lesson about talking to people in very high places: avoid the hypothetical question, of the sort that usually begins, 'What if . . .' and then departs into some fanciful situation that never happened and never will. That type of question can be asked of creative people, for whom imaginary situations are intriguing, but practical, crisp people dismiss it as a waste of time."

When the subject is inventive and in the mood, however, hypothetical questions are fecund. Kenneth Tynan asked Richard Burton, "If you had your life to live over again, would you change anything?"—a question that is as worn out as vaudeville.

But Burton's reply was fresh and revealing: "I'd like to be born the son of a duke with 90,000 pounds a year, or an enormous estate. . . .

"And I'd like to have the most enormous library, and I'd like to think that I could read those books forever and forever, and die unlamented, unknown, unsung, unhonored—and packed with information."

I have endeavored to give credit to sources throughout the text of this book. Other sources have been invaluable between the lines, however, and I would like to acknowledge the special support and assistance of Russ Larson, Elfrieda Abbe, Ron Kovach, Greg Paul, Kate Broughton, Ric Calabrese, Wally Stamm, Karen Mulvey, Jeff Seglin, Cable Neuhaus, Art Spikol, Christopher Buckley, Susan May, Tom Conuel, Bill Slattery, Diana Knott, Bernhard Debatin, Don Ranly, Jennifer Moeller, Bob Zelnick, Sheryl Jackson, and, in lasting memory, Tom Hunter.

Special thanks to Phil Berwish, my friend and attorney, and to Phil Martin, my guerrilla guide and editor on this endeavor.

Portions of this book were written while I was Scripps Howard Visiting Professional at the E. W. Scripps School of Journalism, Ohio University. My deepest thanks to Dean Kathy Krendl, Director Tom Hodson, Professor Dru Evarts, and colleagues all.

In addition to interviews and correspondence with individuals cited in the text, the following print sources served either as background reading or for text citations along the way. Because some sources are cited in more than one chapter, they are arranged by topic here.—JB

Introduction
David Rakoff, "Questions for Martin Short: Who's Asking?," *New York Times* magazine, June 24, 2001.
Steve Rushin, "Air and Space: Greatly Exaggerated," *Sports Illustrated*, Feb. 8, 1999.
Clea Simon, "For Stamberg, lots to consider," *Boston Globe*, Aug. 2, 2001.

Getting interviews
Shana Alexander, *Talking Woman*, Dell Publishing Co., 1977.
Dave Astor, "Schulz's last newspaper interview?," *Editor & Publisher*, Feb. 21, 2000.
Murray Chass, "An Admission by Rose Would Surprise a Friend," *The New York Times*, Feb 7, 2003.
Barry Golson, ed., *The Playboy Interview*, Playboy Press, 1981.
Lawrence Grobel, *The Hustons*, Scribners, 1989.
Jonathan Kwitny, Letter to editor, *NEWSInc.*, June 1990.
Jeff MacGregor, "Road Rage," *Sports Illustrated*, Oct. 21, 2002.
Barbara Matusik, Bob Woodward profile, *The Washingtonian*, Sept. 1987.
Eric McHenry, "The Boswell of the Blues," *Bostonia* magazine, Fall 2002.
Larry Miller, "Interviewing Celebrities," *Writer's Digest*, July 1988.
James Reston Jr., "'What's In It for Me?'" *The Washingtonian*, Jan. 1990.

Art Spikol, " Quid Pro Quo," *Writer's Digest*, June 1986.

Craig Unger, "Salinger Speaks; Still Inscrutable," *New York Magazine*, July 21, 1980.

Michael Wolff, "Pinch, Power, and the Paper," *New York Magazine*, June 16, 2003.

Richard Zoglin, "The Making of a Scoop," *Time* magazine, Aug. 18, 1986.

The role of the interviewer

Alison Bass, "Shyness doesn't have to be forever," *The Boston Globe*, Sept. 24, 1990.

John Gregory Dunne, *Quintana & Friends*, E.P. Dutton, 1978.

Mark Feeney, "John Chancellor, NBC anchorman, commentator for 23 years; at 68," *The Boston Globe*, July 13, 1996.

Mark Fitzgerald, "For ABC News . . . 'The Price Is Right,'" *Editor & Publisher*, June 12, 1999.

Hal Lancaster, "How to Get Beyond Bashful and Act Like a Careerist," *Wall Street Journal*, Feb. 21, 1995.

Seth Mnookin, "Media Insider: Reporters, Reporting," *Newsweek*, Dec. 30, 2002.

"The Media Interview: 12 Points to Review *Before* the Interview," *Bottom Line Communicator*, Nov. 1988.

Philip Zimbardo, quoted in "An Expert Tells How to Cope With Shyness," *U.S. News & World Report*, Oct. 9, 1978.

Ethics and etiquette

Ian Ayres, "Why Prosecute Linda Tripp?" *The New York Times*, Aug 10, 1999.

Louis Alvin Day, *Ethics in Media Communications: Cases & Controversies*, 4th ed., Louisiana State University, Thomson/Wadsworth, 2003.

Joseph P. Kahn, "How Should the Press Treat Kitty Kelley?" *The Boston Globe*, April 18, 1991.

Michael Kinsley, "Please Don't Quote Me," *Time* magazine, May 13, 1991.

Abbe Wichman, "Veiled Attributions: Familiarity Breeds," *Publishing News*, Nov. 1989.

Dealing with PR

Roger Ailes and Jon Kraushar, "How to Make an Audience Love You," *Working Woman*, Nov. 1990.

Daniel Boorstin, *The Image: A Guide to Pseudo-Events in America*. Vintage, 1961.

David S. Broder, "Presidents Should Speak for Themselves," *The Washington Post*, April 17, 1988.

Jennifer Conlin, "Peggy Siegal Got Married—to Hollywood," *Manhattan Inc.*, December 1988.

David Ellis, "Excuse of the Week," *Time* magazine, Oct. 15, 1990.

"Ghostwriters' No More," *U.S. News & World Report*, Feb. 3, 1986.

Michael Madden, "Hard Times, No Hard Feelings," *The Boston Globe*, Aug. 10, 1990.

Stephen Madden, "Learning to Meet the Press," *M Magazine*, Aug. 1990.

Louis Menand, "The Sweet Smell of Excess: Walter Winchell and the Culture of Gossip," *Manhattan Inc.*, July 1990.

David J. Morrow, "Media Mavens," *Folio's Publishing News*, May 15, 1991.

Lawrence Ragan, "What to do when quoting the plant manager, CEO, or employee," *Bottom Line Communicator*, Feb. 1989.

Martha Smilgis, "The Celebs' Golden Mouthpiece," *Time* magazine, Nov. 27, 1989.

John Taylor, "Trump: The Soap," *New York* magazine, March 5, 1990.

Beth Teitell, "Harvard B School Meets the Press," *Boston Magazine*, April 1990.

Jeffrey Toobin, "Lunch at Martha's," *The New Yorker*, Feb. 3, 2003.

Asking questions

Michael Crowley, "Questions for Ari Fleischer: No More Flak," *The New York Times Magazine*, June 1, 2003.

Malcolm Gladwell, "The New-Boy Network," *The New Yorker*, May 29, 2000.

Tom Hunter, "Self-revelation builds trust in an interview," Effective Communications Group, September 1997.

Susan Lee, "The Kitty Kelley Story," *Mirabella*, April 1991.

Anna Quindlen, "Ignore Them Off the Field," *Newsweek*, Jan. 31, 2000.

B.J. Schecter, "Remembering Will," *Sports Illustrated*, Jan. 20, 2003.

Adele Scheele, "The Power of Small Talk: How to Schmooze Successfully," *Working Woman*, Nov. 1990.

Philip Weiss, "Ellen Barkin Goes Mano a Mano," *Esquire*, April 1991.

Listening

Clay Felker, "Letter from the editor: Earthquakes," *Manhattan, Inc.*, Nov. 1987.

Ellen Graham, "She Has Her Eyes Open, Ears Flappin' and a Nose for News," *Wall Street Journal*, March 18, 1991.

Nina Willdorf, "Aural Pleasures," *New York* magazine, Dec. 23-30, 2002.

Dealing with sources

Pamela Bentley, "Exit Stage Fright," *Working Woman*, Nov. 1990.

Gary Cartwright, "Raving On," *Texas Monthly*, Oct. 1995.

Charles Claffey, "An Interviewer Rates His Interviewees," *The Boston Globe*, Dec. 30, 1988.

Maureen Dowd, "The Prettiest of Them All," *The New York Times*, Dec. 19, 2001.

Alan Feuer, "Long Island Everyman Masters the Sound Bite," *The New York Times*, June 15, 2003.

"The Great Tom Cruise Cover-Up," *Newsweek*, Jan. 29, 1990.

Lin Grensing, "How to Work With the Media," *The Toastmaster*, Jan. 1989.

Lawrence Grobel, "A Star Interview Is Born," *Writer's Digest*, Jan. 1978.

Erik Hedegaard, "New Kid on the Block," *Rolling Stone*, July 10, 2003.

"How *Glamour* gets people to spill those juicy relationship secrets," *Glamour*, Dec. 1998.

Mark Jurkowitz, "Ch. 7 owner plans to sue Herald," *The Boston Globe*, May 16, 2001.

Roger Kahn, "Hard Times for Boomer," *The New York Times*, May 22, 1978.

David Kaplan, "Liars Index," *Adweek*, Feb. 17, 2003.

Marshall Loeb, "Editor's Desk," *Fortune*, Feb. 27, 1989.

Suzy Parker obituary: "Not Just a Glamour Queen, a Model with Attitude," *Time* magazine, June 9, 2003.

Kerry Patterson, Joseph Grenny, Ron McMillan and Al Switzler, *Crucial Conversations: Tools for Talking When Stakes Are High*, McGraw-Hill, 2003.

"Psssst!," *Folio: Magazine*, June 1991.

Stephen C. Rafe, *How to be Prepared to Think on Your Feet*, Harper Business, 1990.

Pamela Sebastian, "A Tip on Touching," *Wall Street Journal*, June 25, 1998.

Alicia Shepard, "The Reporter and the Hit Man," *American Journalism Review*, April 2001.

B.J. Sigesmund, "Fast Chat: A Life in the Closet," *Newsweek*, June 9, 2003.

Joe Strupp, "Going to the source of trouble," *Editor & Publisher*, May 26, 2003.

"When interviewees 'exaggerate,'" *The Week*, May 30, 2003.

Diane White, "When Dapper made me kiss him," *The Boston Globe*, Feb. 16, 1995.

Research, backgrounding, notes and quotes

Jim Cope, "Data Overload: Separating Gold from Garbage," *Hemispheres* magazine, April 1998.

William F. Doherty and Richard J. Connolly, "Tapes Show Zannino Sore Loser in a Game of [Expletive] Poker," *The Boston Globe*, Sept. 24, 1985.

Melissa Hostetler, "More Tips: Internet Searches and Database Development," *ASBPE Editor's Notes*, Nov./Dec. 2000.

Ron Rosenbaum, *The Secret Parts of Fortune: Three Decades of Intense Investigations and Edgy Enthusiasms*, Random House, 2000.

Larry Speakes (with Robert Pack), *Speaking Out*, Scribner's, 1988.

M. L. Stein, "Eastwood Claim vs. Enquirer Upheld," *Editor & Publisher*, Sept. 20, 1997.

Bruce Weber, "A New Kind of Showgirl," *The New York Times*, March 27, 2003.

Telephone & e-mail tactics

Michael Bugeja, "To E or not to E," *Writer's Digest*, April 2003.

Frank DiGiacomo, "The Transom: Muckin' Fergie," *The New York Observer*, Nov. 1, 1999.

Brett Martin, "Don't Call Us, We Won't Call You Either," *O: The Oprah Magazine*, March 2003.

Rudy Maxa, "Call Me Anytime," *The Washingtonian*, Jan. 1990.

Scott Shifrel, "Tokyo: Tough News Capital," *Washington Journalism Review*, Sept. 1988.

Allan Wolper, "To List or Not to List," *Editor & Publisher*, Aug. 13, 2001.

INDEX